Crocheted WREATHS & GARLANDS

Crocheted WREATHS & GARLANDS

35 FLORAL AND FESTIVE DESIGNS TO DECORATE YOUR HOME ALL YEAR ROUND

Kate Eastwood

CICO BOOKS

LONDON NEW YORK

This book is dedicated to Dave, Meg, Beth and Immi – my be-all and end-all. x

Published in 2019 by CICO Books
An imprint of Ryland Peters & Small Ltd
341 E 116th St, New York, NY 10029

www.rylandpeters.com

10 9 8 7 6 5 4 3 2

Text © Kate Eastwood 2019
Design, illustration, and photography ©
CICO Books 2019

A CIP catalog record for this book is
available from the Library of Congress.

ISBN: 978-1-78249-692-2

Printed in China

Editor: Marie Clayton
Designer: Alison Fenton
Photographer: Emma Mitchell
Stylist: Nel Haynes
Illustrator: Stephen Dew

Art director: Sally Powell
Production controller: Mai-Ling Collyer
Publishing manager: Penny Craig
Publisher: Cindy Richards

contents

introduction

Putting together this book has been an absolute joy from start to finish, as it has allowed me to indulge two of my favorite things: my love for all things crochet and a love of my surroundings, both inside and outside. Whether it's to bring the outside season in or to celebrate a festival or special occasion, a garland or wreath offers the perfect way to add a very unique touch to your home.

Wreaths and garlands can be as simple and minimalist or as detailed and abundant as you choose. They can be personalized with favorite colors, flowers, and leaves; what could be better than receiving something beautifully handmade as a birthday, Christmas or thank you present. One of the very first garlands I made was a simple raffia-based garland covered in ivory roses for my daughter's wedding, and there is truly something very special about being able to create something handmade and lasting for a wonderful family celebration.

In this book I have created a wide selection of designs for many different occasions, and I hope it will not only be a book that you come back to many times but will also inspire you to create your own designs for wreaths and garlands that are personal to you. In our home we now have quite a collection that are brought out at different times of the year to decorate our home. There are not many bare shelves or mantelpieces in our house!

I have given each design in the book a skill rating so that, whatever your level of crochet, you will be able to crochet away to your heart's content. One of the simplest designs is the Birthday Wreath (on page 70), as these tiny balloons can be hooked up in no time at all, in any colors —and, with only the smallest amount of yarn being needed, they are a great way of using up all your leftover yarn. For a more detailed make, why not try one of the floral garlands. When making any garland the pleasure of seeing all your work come together, as the individual pieces are stitched into place, is immensely satisfying. If I had to choose a favorite from these designs, I think it would have to be my Gingerbread Garland (see page 109). I could happily have made the tiny little gingerbread men and candy canes for ever, and there may well be a few hung on our family tree this Christmas.

Remember there are no rules with wreaths and garlands—the world is your oyster, whether in color, design, or occasion. Happy crocheting!

CHAPTER 1

SEASONS

As the nights draw in there's something very comforting about the golden fall colors and with this wreath you can bring that cosy feel into your home. The wreath is made up of two different-colored mini pumpkins, oak leaves in varying shades, and three little field mice looking for fall treats.

pumpkin wreath

SKILL RATING: ● ● ○

MATERIALS:

DMC Natura Just Cotton (100% cotton, approx. 169yds/155m in each 1¾oz/50g ball) fingering (4ply) weight yarn
  1 ball each of shades:
    Curry N74 (A)
    Canelle N37 (B)
    Salome N80 (C)
    Safran N47 (D)

US size B/1–C/2 (2.5mm) crochet hook

Yarn needle

Polyester toy stuffing

Thin black fiber tip pen

2 lengths of 2oz (50g) orange raffia

Florist's wire

Pins

Hot glue gun

Ribbon for hanging loop

Needle and thread (optional)

FINISHED MEASUREMENTS:

Each oak leaf: approx. 2¾in (7cm) long

Wreath: 12in (30cm) diameter

GAUGE (TENSION):

15 sts x 15 rows = 2⅜ x 2½in (6 x 6.5cm) working single crochet, using a US size B/1–C/2 (2.5mm) crochet hook.

ABBREVIATIONS:

See page 127.

FOR THE WREATH

OAK LEAF (make 9 in A, 8 in B, 7 in C)

Using A, B or C, ch14.
Round 1: 1sc in 2nd ch from hook, 1sc in each of next 3 ch, 1hdc in each of next 5 ch, 1dc in each of next 3 ch, 5dc in last ch, do not turn, working back down other side of ch, 1dc in each of next 5 ch, 1hdc in each of next 4 ch, 1 sc in each of last 3 ch.
Work in a continuous spiral, do not join.
Round 2:
Lobe 1: 2sc in first st from last round, sl st in next st, (1sc, 1hdc, 1dc) in next st, sl st in next st.
Lobe 2: Sl st in next st, (1sc, 1hdc, 1dc) in next st, sl st in next st.
Lobe 3: Sl st in next st, (1sc, 1hdc, 2dc) in next st, sl st in next st.
Lobe 4: Sl st in next st, (1sc, 1hdc, 2dc) in next st, sl st in next st.
Lobe 5: Sl st in next st, (1sc, 1hdc, 1dc) in next st, (1dc, 1hdc, 1sc) in next st, sl st in each of next 2 sts.
Lobe 6: (Ch2, 1dc, 1hdc) in same st as sl st, (1hdc, 1sc) in next st, sl st in next st.
Lobe 7: Ch2, (1dc, 1hdc) in next st, (1hdc, 1sc) in next st, sl st in next st.
Lobe 8: Sl st in next st, ch2, (1dc, 1hdc) in next st, (1hdc, 1sc) in next st, sl st in next st.
Lobe 9: Sl st in next st, ch1, (2hdc, 1sc) in next st, sl st in next st.
Stem: Ch5, sl st in 2nd ch from hook, sl st in each of next 3 ch, sl st in base of stem.
Fasten off.

PUMPKIN (make 4 in D, 2 in B)

Using D or B, ch16.
Row 1: 1sc in 2nd ch from hook, 1sc in each ch to end. *15 sts.*
Row 2: Ch1, 1sc BLO in each st to end.
Rows 3 to 28: Rep row 2.
Fasten off, leaving a long tail.

STALK (make one for each pumpkin in contrast color)

Using D or B, ch8.
Row 1: 1sc in 2nd ch from hook, 1sc in each ch to end. *7 sts.*
Row 2: 1sc in each of first 6 sts, sl st in last st.
Row 3: Sl st in first st, 1sc in each of next 6 sts.
Row 4: Ch1, 1sc in each of first 4 sts, sl st in each of last 2 sts.
Fasten off, leaving a long tail.

MOUSE (make 2 in C, 1 in B)

Round 1: Using B or C, make a magic ring, 4sc into the ring.

Work in a continuous spiral. PM in last st and move up as each round is finished.

Round 2: [1sc, 2sc in next st] twice. *6 sts.*

Round 3: [1sc, 2sc in next st] 3 times. *9 sts.*

Round 4: 1sc in each st to end.

Round 5 (ears): (Sl st, ch2, 1dc, ch2, sl st) in FLO of first st, 1sc in both loops of next st, (sl st, ch2, 1dc, ch2, sl st) in FLO of next st, 1sc in both loops of each of last 6 sts.

Round 6: 2sc in BLO behind ear, 1sc in both loops of next st, 2sc in BLO behind second ear, working in both loops, 1sc in each of next 2 sts, 2sc in next st, 1sc in next st, 2sc in each of next 2 sts. *14 sts.*

Rounds 7 to 9: 1sc in each st to end.

Round 10: 1sc in each of first 8 sts, sc2tog, 1sc, sc2tog, 1sc. *12 sts.*

Round 11: [Sc2tog, 1sc] 4 times. *8 sts.*

Stuff the mouse.

Round 12: [Sc2tog] to end.

Fasten off but do not cut yarn, ch20 for tail.

Fasten off.

MAKING UP AND FINISHING

Block the oak leaves.

Fold the pumpkin RS together, re-join the matching yarn and join two short edges with an sc seam.

Fasten off. Using the long tail in a yarn needle, run a gathering thread along one of the long edges. Pull up and finish off, sewing a few extra stitches across the bottom of the pumpkin to close the hole securely.

Run another gathering thread around the other edge, pull up slightly and stuff the pumpkin. Finish closing up the hole, leaving a small hole open for the stalk.

Using the long tail in a yarn needle, join the two long edges of the stalk—the narrower part of the stalk is the top. Then thread the needle right through the pumpkin, from top to bottom, so that the stalk fits into the hole left in the pumpkin. Secure the stalk with a few stitches, pulling it down quite tightly so that you create an indent in the top of the pumpkin. Fasten off.

Dot 2 eyes on the mouse with a thin black fiber tip pen.

Make up the wreath base with the florist's wire and raffia, as explained on page 125. Lay the wreath on a flat surface and use blocking pins to position the oak leaves and pumpkins where you want them to be. Glue firmly in place with a hot glue gun.

Position the mice and glue in place.

To finish off the wreath, add a hanging loop at the top of the wreath and stitch or glue in place.

This lovely garland will bring all the golden colors of the fall into your home and looks perfect hung on any shelf or fireplace. With its raffia base, it can be made to whatever length you like and can be shaped to create two or more swags.

fall garland

FOR THE WREATH

PINECONE (make 8 in A, 4 in B)
Using A or B, ch61.
Row 1: 1sc in 2nd ch from hook, 1sc in each ch to end, turn. *60 sc.*
Row 2: Ch1, [MB, sl st in next st] 4 times, 1sc in each of next 52 sts, turn.
Row 3: Ch1, 1sc in each of first 52 sts, turn, leaving rem sts unworked. *52 sts.*
Row 4: Ch1, [MB, sl st in next st] 5 times, 1sc in each of next 42 sts, turn.
Row 5: Ch1, 1sc in each of first 42 sts, turn, leaving rem sts unworked. *42 sts.*
Row 6: Ch1, [MB, sl st in next st] 6 times, 1sc in each of next 30 sts, turn.
Row 7: Ch1, 1sc in each of next 30 sts, turn, leaving rem sts unworked. *30 sts.*
Row 8: Ch1, [MB, sl st in next st] 7 times, 1sc in each of next 16 sts, turn.
Row 9: Ch1, 1sc in each of next 16 sts, turn, leaving rem sts unworked. *16 sts.*
Row 10: Ch1, [MB, sl st in next st] 8 times.
Fasten off, leaving a long end.

SKILL RATING: ● ● ○

MATERIALS:
Schachenmayr Catania (100% cotton, approx. 137yds/125m per 1¾oz/50g ball) sport (5 ply) weight yarn
  2 balls each of shades:
    Kamel 0179 (A)
    Zimt 0383 (B)

  1 ball each of shades:
    Gold 0249 (C)
    Olive 0395 (D)
    Apfel 0205 (E)

US size B/1–C/2 (2.5mm) crochet hook

Small amount of polyester toy stuffing

Stitch marker

Yarn needle

3 lengths of 2oz (50g) Raffia

Florist's wire

Pins

Needle and thread

Coordinating ribbon for bows

Thin string for hanging loops

FINISHED MEASUREMENTS:
Oak leaf: 3¼in (8cm) long
Garland: approx. 56in (140cm) long

GAUGE (TENSION):
15 sts x 15 rows = 2½in (6.5cm) square working single crochet, using a US size B/1–C/2 (2.5mm) crochet hook.

ABBREVIATIONS:
See page 127.

SPECIAL ABBREVIATION:
MB (make bobble): insert hook in next st, [yoh, pull a loop through] 5 times, yoh and pull through all loops on hook, ch1 to complete bobble

MAPLE LEAF (make 7 in B, 11 in C)

Round 1: Using B or C, make a magic ring, 6hdc into the ring, join with a sl st in first st.

Round 2: Ch1 (does not count as st throughout), 2hdc in each of first 5 sts only (arch shape formed), turn. *10 sts.*

Round 3: Ch1, 1hdc in each of next 3 sts, 2dc in next st, 2tr in each of next 2 sts, 2dc in next st, 1hdc in each of next 3 sts. *14 sts.*

Now cont around along bottom of arch, (1hdc, 1sc) in same st as last st, 1sc in next st (left unworked from round 1), (1sc, 1hdc) in next st (same st as first hdc of round 3), join with a sl st in first st of round 3.

Round 4:

Leaflet 1: Ch4, 1tr in next st of leaf center, ch2, sl st in 2nd ch from hook, 1sc in next ch, cont working downward, working over the tr and into initial 4-ch, 1dc in next ch, 1tr in each of next 2 ch, skip last ch of 4-ch, sl st in next st of leaf center.

Leaflet 2: Sl st in next st of leaf center, ch5, 1dtr in next st of leaf center, ch3, work back down ch, working over the dtr and into initial 5-ch when you reach it as in leaflet 1, sl st in first ch, 1sc, 1hdc, 1dc, 1tr in each of next 3 ch, skip last ch, sl st in next st of leaf center.

Leaflet 3: Sl st in next st of leaf center, ch8, 1dtr in next st of leaf center, ch4, work back down ch, working over the dtr and into initial 8-ch when you reach it, sl st in each of first 2 ch, 1sc in each of next 2 ch, 1hdc in each of next 2 ch, 1dc in each of next 2 ch, 1tr, 1dtr, skip last 2 ch, skip one st of leaf center, sl st in next st of leaf center.

Leaflet 4: Rep leaflet 2.

Leaflet 5: Rep leaflet 1.

Fasten off.

OAK LEAF (make 11 in C, 18 in D)
Using C or D, ch14.
Round 1: 1sc in 2nd ch from hook, 1sc in each of next 3ch, 1hdc in each of next 5 ch, 1dc in each of next 3 ch, 5dc in last ch, do not turn, working back down other side of ch, 1dc in each of next 5 ch, 1hdc in each of next 4 ch, 1sc in each of last 3 ch, join with a sl st in first st.
Round 2:
Lobe 1: 2sc in first st, sl st in next st, (1sc, 1hdc, 1dc) in next st, sl st in next st.
Lobe 2: Sl st in next sl, (1sc, 1hdc, 1dc) in next st, sl st in next st.
Lobe 3: Sl st in next st, (1sc, 1hdc, 2dc) in next st, sl st in next st.
Lobe 4: Sl st in next st, (1sc, 1hdc, 2dc) in next st, sl st in next st.
Lobe 5: Sl st in next st, (1sc, 1hdc, 1dc) in next st, (1dc, 1hdc, 1sc) in next st, sl st in each of next 2 sts.
Lobe 6: (Ch2, 1dc, 1hdc) in same st as sl st, (1hdc, 1sc) in next st, sl st in next st.
Lobe 7: Ch2, (1dc, 1hdc, sl st) in next st, sl st in next st.
Lobe 8: (Sl st, ch2) in next st, (1dc, 1hdc) in next st, (1hdc, 1sc) in next st, sl st in next st.
Lobe 9: (Sl st, ch1) in next st, 2hdc in next st, 1sc, sl st in next st.
Sl st in base of leaf, ch5, sl st in each of 5 ch, sl st in base of leaf.
Fasten off.

ACORN CUP (make 19)
Round 1: Using D, make a magic ring, 5sc into the ring. Work in a continuous spiral. PM in last st and move up as each round is finished.
Round 2: 2sc in each st to end. *10 sts.*
Round 3: *1sc, 2sc in next st; rep from * to end. *15 sts.*
Round 4: *1sc in each of next 2 sts, 2sc in next st; rep from * to end. *20 sts.*
Round 5: *1sc in each of next 2 sts, sc2tog; rep to end, join with a sl st in first st. *15 sts.*
Fasten off.

ACORN (make 19)
Round 1: Using E, make a magic ring, 4sc into the ring. Work in a continuous spiral. PM in last st and move up as each round is finished.
Round 2: 2sc in each st to end. *8 sts.*
Round 3: *1sc, 2sc in next st; rep from * to end. *12 sts.*
Rounds 4 to 7: 1sc in each st to end.
Fasten off.

MAKING UP AND FINISHING

Block each leaf.

To complete the pinecone, starting at the wider end roll up the length of crochet to form the pinecone shape and use the yarn tail to stitch it firmly in place.

Stuff each acorn, then place it inside a cup and stitch in place. Fasten off.

Make up the garland base with the florist's wire and raffia, as explained on page 125. Lay your raffia base on a flat surface and use blocking pins to position your leaves, pinecones, and acorns where you want them to be. Stitch them all securely in place by sewing them onto the raffia using a needle and thread.

Add a bow in a coordinating ribbon at each end and in the center of the garland. Tie small string loops at the back of the garland for hanging.

For a change from chocolate eggs at Easter, try some pretty spotted crocheted ones instead! The two sizes of egg in bright spring colors and the large and small ivy leaves in green will welcome in those warmer days.

easter egg wreath

SKILL RATING: ● ○ ○

MATERIALS:

Rowan Summerlite 4ply (100% cotton, approx. 191yds/175m per 1¾oz/50g ball) fingering (4 ply) weight yarn
   1 ball each of shades:
      Sandstone 435 (A)
      Ecru 436 (B)
      Pinched Pink 426 (C)

Rowan Cotton Glace (100% cotton, approx. 125yds/115m per 1¾oz/50g ball) light worsted (DK) weight yarn
   1 ball of Shoot 814 (D)

US size B/1–C/2 (2.5mm) crochet hook

Yarn needle

Stitch marker

1½in (40mm) polystyrene eggs (optional)

1¼in (30mm) polystyrene eggs (optional)

Polyester toy stuffing (if not using polystyrene eggs)

10in (25cm) diameter pale wicker wreath

Pins

Hot glue gun

Ribbon

FINISHED MEASUREMENTS:
Wreath: 10in (25cm) diameter

GAUGE (TENSION):
15 sts x 15 rows = 2⅜in (6cm) square working single crochet, using a US size B/1–C/2 (2.5mm) crochet hook.

ABBREVIATIONS:
See page 127.

FOR THE WREATH

LARGE IVY LEAF (make 5 in D)

Round 1: Using D, make a magic ring, 5sc into the ring.
Work in a continuous spiral. PM in last st and move up as each round is finished.
Round 2: 2sc in each st to end. *10 sc.*
Round 3: *1sc, 2sc in next st; rep from * to end, join with a sl st in first st. *15 sc.*
Point 1: Ch4, sl st in 2nd ch from hook, 1sc, 1hdc, skip next st of center, sl st in next st.
Point 2: Ch5, sl st in 2nd ch from hook, 1sc, 1hdc, 1dc, skip next st of center, sl st in next st.
Point 3: Ch7, sl st in 2nd ch from hook, 1sc, 1hdc, 1dc, 1tr, 1dtr, skip 2 sts of center, sl st in next st of center.
Point 4: Rep point 2.
Point 5: Rep point 1.
Stem: Sl st in next st, ch5, sl st in 2nd ch from hook, sl st in each of next 3 ch, sl st in base of 5-ch.
Fasten off.

SMALL IVY LEAF (make 8 in D)

Round 1: Using D, make a magic ring, 4sc into the ring.
Work in a continuous spiral. PM in last st and move up as each round is finished.
Round 2: 2sc in each st to end. *8 sc.*
Round 3: *1sc, 2sc in next st; rep from * to end, join with a sl st in first st. *12 sc.*
Point 1: Ch3, sl st in 2nd ch from hook, 1sc, sl st in next st.
Point 2: Ch4, sl st in 2nd ch from hook, 1sc, 1hdc, skip next st of center, sl st in next st.
Point 3: Ch6, sl st in 2nd ch from hook, 1sc, 1hdc, 1dc, 1tr, skip 2 sts of center, sl st in next st.
Point 4: Rep point 2.
Point 5: Rep point 1.
Stem: Sl st in next st, ch5, sl st in 2nd ch from hook, sl st in each of next 3 ch, sl st in base of 5-ch.
Fasten off.

||||||||||||||||||||||||||||||||||||||||||||||||||||||

The eggs on the wreath can be made in two
different ways—either by adding a
polystyrene egg halfway through or by
stuffing the egg with toy stuffing. Both ways
work equally well.

LARGE EGG (make 3 in A, 1 in B, 1 in C)

Round 1: Using A, B or C, make a magic ring, 4sc into the ring.

Work in a continuous spiral. PM in last st and move up as each round is finished.

Round 2: 2sc in each st to end. *8 sts.*

Round 3: *1sc, 2sc in next st; rep from * to end. *12 sts.*

Round 4: *1sc in each of next 2 sts, 2sc in next st; rep from * to end. *16 sts.*

Round 5: *1sc in each of next 3 sts, 2sc in next st; rep from * to end. *20 sts.*

Rounds 6 and 7: 1sc in each st to end. *20 sts.*

Round 8: *1sc in each of next 4 sts, 2sc in next st; rep from * to end. *24 sts.*

Rounds 9 to 12: 1sc in each st to end.

Insert polystyrene egg (optional).

Round 13: *1sc in each of next 4 sts, sc2tog; rep from * to end. *20 sts.*

Round 14: *1sc in each of next 3 sts, sc2tog; rep from * to end. *16 sts.*

Round 15: *1sc in each of next 2 sts, sc2tog; rep from * to end. *12 sts.*

If not using polystyrene egg, insert stuffing.

Round 16: *1sc, sc2tog; rep from * to end. *8 sts.*

Round 17: [Sc2tog] to end.

Fasten off.

SMALL EGG (make 1 in B, 2 in C)

Round 1: Using B or C, make a magic ring, 4sc into the ring.

Work in a continuous spiral. PM in last st and move up as each round is finished.

Round 2: 2sc in each st to end. *8 sts.*

Round 3: *1sc, 2sc in next st; rep from * to end. *12 sts.*

Round 4: *1sc in each of next 2 sts, 2sc in next st; rep from * to end. *16 sts.*

Rounds 5 and 6: 1sc in each st to end.

Round 7: *1sc in each of next 3 sts, 2sc in next st; rep from * to end. *20 sts.*

Round 8: *1sc in each of next 4 sts, 2sc in next st; rep from * to end. *24 sts.*

Rounds 9 and 10: 1sc in each st. *24 sts.*

Insert polystyrene egg (optional).

Round 11: *1sc in each of next 4 sts, sc2tog; rep from * to end. *20 sts.*

Round 12: *1sc in each of next 3 sts, sc2tog; rep from * to end. *16 sts.*

Round 13: *1sc in each of next 2 sts, sc2tog; rep from * to end. *12 sts.*

If not using polystyrene egg, insert stuffing.

Round 14: *1sc, sc2tog; rep from * to end. *8 sts.*

Round 15: [Sc2tog] to end.

Fasten off.

MAKING UP AND FINISHING

Block the ivy leaves.

To finish the eggs, work some French knots (see page 123) all over each egg in contrasting colors.

Lay the wreath on a flat surface and use blocking pins to position and pin the blocked ivy leaves and eggs where you want them to be. Glue firmly in place with a hot glue gun.

To finish off the wreath, stitch or glue a coordinating ribbon and hanging loop at the top.

This flowery garland will bring a little bit of the outside in and add some vibrant color to your fireplace or mantelpiece during the summer months. With its raffia base, it can be made to whatever length you like and can be shaped to create two or more swags.

summer flower garland

SKILL RATING: ● ● ○

MATERIALS:

Schachenmayr Catania (100% cotton, approx. 136yds/125m per 1¾oz/50g ball) sport (5 ply) weight yarn
  1 ball each of shades:
    Anis 0245 (A)
    Rosa 0246 (B)
    Marsalarot 0396 (C)
    Kamel 0179 (D)
    Apfel 0205 (E)

US size B/1–C/2 (2.5mm) crochet hook

Yarn needle

Florist's wire

3 lengths of 2oz (50g) raffia

Pins

Needle and thread

FINISHED MEASUREMENTS:

Each six-petal spike flower: approx. 1¾in (4.5cm) wide

Garland: approx. 50in (127cm) long

GAUGE (TENSION):

15 sts x 15 rows = 2½in (6.5cm) square working single crochet, using a US size B/1–C/2 (2.5mm) crochet hook.

ABBREVIATIONS:

See page 127.

FOR THE GARLAND

SIX-PETAL SPIKE FLOWER (make 20)

Round 1: Using A, make a magic ring, 6sc into the ring.
Work in a continuous spiral, do not join.
Round 2: 2sc in each st to end, join with a sl st in first st. *12 sts.*
Round 3: *Ch1, 2dc in same st as sl st, ch3, sl st in 3rd ch from hook, 2dc in next st, ch1, sl st in same st, sl st in next st; rep from * 5 more times around center (6 petals), sl st in base of first petal.
Fasten off A.

LARGE FIVE-PETAL FLOWER (make 24 in combination of B, C and D)

Round 1: Using B, C or D, make a magic ring, 5sc into the ring.
Work in a continuous spiral, do not join.
Round 2: 2sc in each st around, join with a sl st in first st. *10 sts.*
Fasten off.
Round 3: Join in B, C or D contrast color with a sl st, *ch3, 2dc in same st as sl st, 2dc in next st, ch3, sl st in same st, sl st in next st; rep from * 4 more times around center (5 petals), sl st in base of first petal.
Fasten off.

SMALL 5-PETAL FLOWER (make 24 in combination B, C and D)

Round 1: Using B, C or D, make a magic ring, 5sc into the ring, join with a sl st in first st.
Fasten off.
Round 2: Join in B, C or D contrast color with a sl st, *(ch2, 1 dc, ch2, sl st) in same st as sl st, sl st in next st; rep from * 4 more times around center (5 petals), ending last petal with sl st in base of first petal.
Fasten off.

LARGE LEAF (make 16)

Using E, ch12.

Round 1: Sl st in 2nd ch from hook, 1sc, 1hdc in each of next 2 ch, 1dc, 2dc in the next ch, 1dc, 1hdc in each of next
2 ch, 1sc in each of last 2 ch, do not turn, ch1, working back down other side of ch, 1sc in each of first 2 ch, 1hdc in each of next 2 ch, 1dc, 2dc in next ch, 1dc, 1hdc in each of next 2 ch, 1sc, sl st in last ch, join with a sl st in beg 1-ch.

Round 2 (textured edge): *Sl st in next st, ch1; rep from * around edge of leaf, join with a sl st in first st.
Fasten off.

SMALL LEAF (make 20)

Using E, ch10.

Round 1: Sl st in 2nd ch from hook, 1sc, 1hdc, 1dc in each of next 3 ch, 1hdc, 1sc in each of last 2 ch, do not turn, ch1, working back down other side of ch, 1sc in each of first 2 ch, 1hdc, 1dc in each of next 3 ch, 1hdc, 1sc, sl st in last ch, join with a sl st in beg 1-ch.
Fasten off.

MAKING UP AND FINISHING

Block each flower and leaf.

To finish the six-petal spike flower, work a French knot (see page 123) in the center of the flower in a contrast color, and another 6 French knots around the center one.

Make up the garland base with the florist's wire and raffia, as explained on page 125. Lay your base on a flat surface. Use blocking pins to position your blocked flowers and leaves where you want them to be. Stitch the flowers and leaves securely in place by sewing them on to the raffia using a needle and thread.

This alternative Easter garland is made up of chicken's eggs and fresh spring carrots! Each item is tied onto a rustic piece of rope for a simple, fresh look—perfect for hanging in your kitchen.

simple easter garland

SKILL RATING: ● ● ●

MATERIALS:

Rowan Summerlite DK (100% cotton, approx. 142yds/130m per 1¾oz/50g ball) light worsted (DK) weight yarn
  1 ball each of shades:
    Linen 460 (A)
    Pear 463 (B)
    Cantaloupe 456 (C)

US size B/1–C/2 (2.5mm) crochet hook

Stitch marker

Polyester toy stuffing

Yarn needle

11 short lengths of thin string

60in (1.5m) of cord or thin rope

6 short lengths of green ribbon

FINISHED MEASUREMENTS:

Carrot: approx. 4in (10cm) long

Egg: approx. 2in (5cm) long

Garland: approx. 52in (130cm) long

GAUGE (TENSION):

15 sts x 15 rows = 2⅜in (6cm) square working single crochet, using a US size B/1–C/2 (2.5mm) crochet hook.

ABBREVIATIONS:

See page 127.

FOR THE GARLAND

EGG (make 7)

Round 1: Using A, make a magic ring, 4sc into the ring.
Work in a continuous spiral. PM in last st and move up as each round is finished.
Round 2: 2sc in each st to end. *8 sts.*
Round 3: *1sc, 2sc in next st; rep from * to end. *12 sts.*
Round 4: *1sc in each of next 2 sts, 2sc in next st; rep from * to end. *16 sts.*
Rounds 5 and 6: 1sc in each st to end.
Round 7: *1sc in each of next 3 sts, 2sc in next st; rep from * to end. *20 sts.*
Round 8: *1sc in each of next 4 sts, 2sc in next st; rep from * to end. *24 sts.*
Rounds 9 and 10: 1sc in each st to end.
Stuff top of egg.
Round 11: *1sc in each of next 4 sts, sc2tog; rep from * to end. *20 sts.*
Round 12: *1sc in each of next 3 sts, sc2tog; rep from * to end. *16 sts.*
Round 13: *1sc in each of next 2 sts, sc2tog; rep from * to end. *12 sts.*
Round 14: *1sc, sc2tog; rep from * to end. *8 sts.*
Finish stuffing egg.
Round 15: [Sc2tog] to end.
Fasten off.

CARROT (make 5)

Round 1: Using C, make a magic ring, 4sc into the ring.
Work in a continuous spiral. PM in last st and move up as each round is finished.
Round 2: *1sc, 2sc in next st; rep from * to end. *6 sts.*
Round 3: 1sc in each st to end.
Round 4: *1sc, 2sc in next st; rep from * to end. *9 sts.*
Round 5: 1sc in each st to end.
Round 6: *1sc, 2sc in next st; rep from * 3 more times, 1sc. *13 sts.*
Round 7: 1sc in each st to end.
Round 8: *1sc in each of next 2 sts, 2sc in next st; rep from * 3 more times, 2sc in next st. *18 sts.*
Round 9: 1sc in each st to end.
Round 10: *1sc in each of next 3 sts, 2sc in next st; rep from * 3 more times, 1sc in each of next 2 sts. *22 sts.*
Rounds 11 to 18: 1sc in each st to end.
Round 19: *2sc, sc2tog; rep from * 4 more times, 2sc. *17 sts.*
Round 20: *1sc, sc2tog; rep from * 4 more times, 2sc. *12 sts.*
Stuff carrot.
Round 21: [Sc2tog] to end. *6 sts.*

Gather up rem hole to close, then fasten off.
To finish the carrot, join B to center top of carrot with a
sl st, *ch11, sl st in each of next 11 ch, join with a sl st in
center top of carrot; rep from * 4 more times.
Fasten off.

MAKING UP AND FINISHING

Thread a length of thin string into the top of each carrot
and egg and hang each item onto the length of rope to
form your garland. Tie a small bow in green ribbon above
each egg.

MATERIALS:

Rowan Handknit Cotton (100% cotton, approx. 93yds/85m per 1¾oz/50g ball) worsted (Aran) weight yarn
  1 ball each of shades:
    Rosso 215 (A)
    Gooseberry 219 (B)

Rowan Summerlite 4 ply (100% cotton, approx. 191yds/175m per 1¾oz/50g ball) fingering (4 ply) weight yarn
  1 ball each of shades:
    Ecru 436 (C)
    Buttermilk 421 (D)

US size C/2–D/3 (3mm) and US size B/1–C/2 (2.5mm) crochet hooks

Polyester toy stuffing

Stitch marker

Yarn needle

10in (25cm) diameter wicker wreath

Pins

Hot glue gun

Ribbon for hanging loop

FINISHED MEASUREMENTS:

Each large leaf: 1¾in (4.5cm)

Wreath: 10in (25cm) diameter

GAUGE (TENSION):

15 sts x 15 rows = 2¾in (7cm) square working single crochet, using a US size C/2–D/3 (3mm) crochet hook and Rowan Handknit Cotton.

15 sts x 15 rows = 2⅜in (6cm) square working single crochet, using a US size B/1–C/2 (2.5mm) crochet hook and Rowan Summerlite DK.

ABBREVIATIONS:

See page 127.

SPECIAL ABBREVIATION:

make petal: *yoh, insert hook in st, yoh and pull through st, yoh and pull through 2 loops on hook; rep from * 2 more times in same st, yoh, pull through all 4 loops on hook

A bowl of fresh strawberries is so synonymous with warm summer days; this wreath captures that feeling and allows you to bring it into your home. From the bright red of the strawberries to the zingy green leaves, this wreath will have you dreaming of summer all year round.

strawberry summer wreath

FOR THE WREATH

STRAWBERRY (make 8)

Round 1: Using A and US size C/2–D/3 (3mm) hook, make a magic ring, 4sc into the ring.
Work in a continuous spiral. PM in last st and move up as each round is finished.
Round 2: *1sc, 2sc in next st; rep from * to end. *6 sts.*
Round 3: 1sc in each st to end.
Round 4: *1sc, 2sc in next st; rep from * to end. *9 sts.*
Round 5: *1sc in each of next 2 sts, 2sc in next st; rep from * to end. *12 sts.*
Round 6: 1sc in each st to end.
Round 7: *1sc in each of next 3 sts, 2sc in next st; rep from * to end. *15 sts.*
Round 8: 1sc in each st to end.
Round 9: *1sc in each of next 3 sts, sc2tog; rep from * to end. *12 sts.*
Stuff the strawberry.
Round 10: [Sc2tog] to end. *6 sts.*
Fasten off, using long end to gather and close hole.

STRAWBERRY TOP (make 8)

Round 1: Using B and US size C/2–D/3 (3mm) hook, make a magic ring, 5sc into the ring, join with a sl st in first st.
Round 2: *Ch5, sl st in each of next 5 ch, sl st in next st of center; rep from * 4 times around center (5 leaves), ending last leaf with sl st in base of first leaf.
Fasten off.

STRAWBERRY FLOWER (make 15)

Round 1: Using D and US size B/1–C/2 (2.5mm) hook, make a magic ring, 5hdc into the ring, join with a sl st in first st.
Fasten off.
Round 2: Join in C with a sl st, *ch3, make petal in same st as sl st, ch3, sl st in same st as petal, sl st in next st; rep from * 4 times around center (5 petals), ending last petal with sl st in base of first petal.
Fasten off.

LARGE LEAF (make 10)

Using B and US size C/2–D/3 (3mm) hook, ch9.

Round 1: 1sc in first ch, 1hdc, 1dc, 1tr in each of next 2 ch, 1dc, 1hdc, 1sc, 2sc in last ch, do not turn, working back down other side of ch, 1hdc, 1dc, 1tr in each of next 2 ch, 1dc, 1hdc, 1sc, skip last ch, join with a sl st in first st.

Round 2: Ch1, *sl st in next st, ch3; rep from * around leaf, join with a sl st in first st.

Fasten off.

SMALL LEAF (make 9)

Using B and US size C/2–D/3 (3mm) hook, ch7.

Round 1: 1sc in first ch, 1hdc, 1dc in each of next 2 ch, 1hdc, 1sc, 2sc in last ch, do not turn, working back down other side of ch, 1hdc, 1dc in each of next 2 ch, 1hdc, 1sc, skip last ch, join with a sl st in first st.

Round 2: Ch1, *sl st in next st, ch2; rep from * around leaf, join with a sl st in first st.

Fasten off.

MAKING UP AND FINISHING

To complete the strawberries sew a top onto each one. Then using C, stitch small running stitches all over the fruit to represent the seeds.

Block the flowers and leaves.

Lay the wreath on a flat surface and use blocking pins to position the flowers, leaves and strawberries where you want them to be. Glue firmly in place with a hot glue gun.

To finish off the wreath add a hanging loop and bow at the top of the wreath and stitch or glue in place.

harvest wreath

A bountiful harvest in late summer signals the start of fall and the evenings beginning to draw in. This wreath is bursting with ripe apples, blackberries, and plump heads of corn. The base used is a large circular twig wreath, perfect for adorning a door or to hang above the fireplace.

SKILL RATING: ● ● ○

MATERIALS:
Rowan Cotton Glace (100% cotton, approx. 125yds/115m per 1¾oz/50g ball) light worsted (DK) weight yarn
  1 ball each of shades:
    Ochre 833 (A)
    Blood Orange 445 (B)
    Pine 869 (C)
    Poppy 741 (D)
    Toffee 843 (E)
    Mineral 856 (F)

US size C/2–D/3 (3mm) and US size B/1 (2mm) crochet hooks

Stitch marker

Yarn needle

Polyester toy stuffing

Thin string for tying the wheat together

16in (40cm) diameter twig wreath

Pins

Hot glue gun

Ribbon for hanging loop

FINISHED MEASUREMENTS:
Each plain leaf: approx. 1¾in (4.5cm) long

Wreath: approx. 16in (40cm) diameter

GAUGE (TENSION):
15 sts x 15 rows = 2¾ x 2½in (7 x 6.5cm) working single crochet, using a US size C/2–D/3 (3mm) crochet hook

ABBREVIATIONS:
See page 127.

FOR THE WREATH
TEXTURED LEAF (make 12 in E, 12 in F)
Using E or F and US size C/2–D/3 (3mm) hook, ch10.
Round 1: 1sc in 2nd ch from hook, 1sc in next ch, 1hdc in each of next 4 ch, 1sc in each of next 2 ch, 2sc in last ch, do not turn, working back down other side of ch, 1sc in each of next 2 ch, 1hdc in each of next 4 ch, 1sc in each of next 2 ch, join with a sl st in first st.
Round 2: (Ch1, sl st) in each st to top of leaf, ch3, sl st in 3rd ch from hook, (sl st, ch1) in each st to base of leaf, join with a sl st in first st. Fasten off.

PLAIN LEAF (make 8 in A, 8 in C, 6 in F)
Using A, C or F and US size C/2–D/3 (3mm) hook, ch10.
Round 1: 1sc in 2nd ch from hook, 1sc in next ch, 1hdc in each of next 4 ch, 1sc in each of next 2 ch, 2sc in last ch, do not turn, working back down other side of ch, 1sc in each of next 2 ch, 1hdc in each of next 4 ch, 1sc in each of next 2 ch, join with a sl st in first st.
Round 2: Ch1, sl st in each st to top of leaf, ch2 at top of leaf, sl st in 2nd ch from hook, sl st in each st to base of leaf, join with a sl st in first st. Fasten off.

BLACKBERRY (make 18)

Round 1: Using B and US size C/2–D/3 (3mm) hook, make a magic ring, 4sc into the ring.
Work in a continuous spiral. PM in last st and move up as each round is finished.
Round 2: *1sc, 2sc in next st; rep from * to end. *6 sts.*
Round 3: 1sc in each st to end.
Round 4: *1sc, 2sc in next st; rep from * to end. *9 sts.*
Round 5: [Sc2tog] 4 times, 1sc. *5 sts.*
Stuff the blackberry.
Round 6: [Sc2tog] twice, 1 sc. *3 sts.*
Fasten off, using long end to gather and close hole.

BLACKBERRY STALK (make 18)

Using C and US size C/2–D/3 (3mm) hook, ch4.
Fasten off.

WHEAT (make 13)

Round 1: Using A and US size C/2–D/3 (3mm) hook, make a magic ring, 3sc into the ring.
Work in a continuous spiral. PM in last st and move up as each round is finished.
Round 2: 2sc in each st to end. *6 sts.*
Rounds 3 to 10: 1sc in each st to end.
Round 11: Removing marker as you pass it, sc2tog, 1sc in each of next 5 sts, stuff wheat, [sc2tog] twice.
Change to US size B/1 (2mm) hook, ch18.
Fasten off.

APPLE (make 3 in B, 6 in D)

Round 1: Using B or D and US size C/2–D/3 (3mm) hook, make a magic ring, 6sc into the ring.
Work in a continuous spiral. PM in last st and move up as each round is finished.
Round 2: 2sc in each st to end. *12 sts.*
Round 3: *1sc, 2sc in next st; rep from * to end. *18 sts.*
Round 4: 1sc in each st to end.
Round 5: *1sc in each of next 2 sts, 2sc in next st; rep from * to end. *24 sts.*
Round 6: *1sc in each of next 3 sts, 2sc in next st; rep from * to end. *30 sts.*
Rounds 7 and 8: 1sc in each st to end.
Round 9: *1sc in each of next 3 sts, sc2tog; rep from * to end. *24 sts.*
Round 10: *1sc in each of next 2 sts, sc2tog; rep from * to end. *18 sts.*

Round 11: *1sc in next st, sc2tog; rep from * to end. *12 sts.*
Stuff apple.
Round 12: 1sc in each st to end.
Round 13: [Sc2tog] to end. *6 sts.*
Fasten off, using long end to gather and close hole.

APPLE LEAF (make 14)

Using C and US size B/1 (2mm) hook, ch6.
Round 1: Sl st in first ch, 1sc, 1hdc in each of next 2 ch, 1sc in each of last 2 ch, do not turn, working back down other side of ch, skip first ch, 1hdc in each of next 2 ch, 1sc, sl st in next ch, join with a sl st in first st.
Fasten off.

APPLE STALK (make 9)

Using E and US size C/2–D/3 (3mm) hook, ch6, sl st in each ch to end.
Fasten off.

MAKING UP AND FINISHING

Block the leaves.

To finish the blackberry, attach the stalk and finish off the ends.

Tie small bundles of three to four stalks of wheat together with thin string.

To finish the apple, thread the remaining yarn from the top through to the bottom and then from the bottom of the apple through to the top. Do this a couple of times to create an indent at the top of the apple. Fasten off securely. Attach the leaf and stalk, adding two leaves to five of the apples.

Lay the wreath on a flat surface and use blocking pins to position the leaves, apples, blackberries, and wheat ears where you want them to be. Glue firmly in place with a hot glue gun.

To finish off the wreath, add a hanging loop at the top of the wreath and stitch or glue in place.

The first primrose of the year is always such a wonderful sign of the arrival of spring and this tiny wreath is designed to celebrate the coming of the new season. The flowers and leaves are worked in a thin crochet thread on a small hook, making the finished size of the wreath perfectly suited to fill any small space around the home.

mini primrose ring

SKILL RATING: ● ● ●

MATERIALS:

DMC Petra 5 (100% cotton, approx. 437yds/400m per 3½oz/100g ball) crochet thread
1 ball each of shades:
    5742 (A)
    5745 (B)
    5907 (C)

US size B/1 (2mm) crochet hook

6in (15cm) diameter light wicker wreath

Pins

Hot glue gun

Ribbon for a hanging loop

FINISHED MEASUREMENTS:

Each primrose: 1in (2.5cm) wide

Wreath: approx. 6in (15cm) diameter

GAUGE (TENSION):

15 sts x 15 rows = 2 x 1¾in (5 x 4cm) working single crochet, using a US size B/1 (2mm) crochet hook.

ABBREVIATIONS:

See page 127.

SPECIAL ABBREVIATION:

make half-petal: *yoh, insert hook in st, yoh and pull through st, yoh and pull through 2 loops on hook; rep from * 2 more times in same st, yoh, pull through all 4 loops on hook

FOR THE WREATH

PRIMROSE (make 15)

Round 1: Using A, make a magic ring, 5sc into the ring.
Work in a continuous spiral, do not join.
Round 2: 2sc in each st to end, join with a sl st in first st. *10 sts.*
Fasten off.
Round 3: Join in B with a sl st, *ch2, make half-petal in same st as sl st, make half-petal in next st, ch2, sl st in same st, sl st in next st; rep from * 4 times around center (5 petals), ending last petal with sl st in base of first petal.
Fasten off.

LEAF (make 16)

Using C, ch13.
Round 1: 1sc in 2nd ch from hook, 1sc in next ch, 1hdc in each of next 2 ch, 1dc in each of next 4 ch, 1hdc in each of next 2 ch, 1sc, 2sc in last ch, do not turn, working back down other side of ch, 1sc, 1hdc in each of next 2 ch, 1dc in each of next 4 ch, 1hdc in each of next 2 ch, 1sc, skip last ch, join with a sl st in first st.
Round 2: Sl st in each st around edge of leaf, join with a sl st in first st.
Fasten off.

MAKING UP AND FINISHING

Block the primroses and leaves.

Lay the wreath on a flat surface and use blocking pins to position the primroses and leaves where you want them to be. Glue firmly in place with a hot glue gun.

To finish off the wreath, add a hanging loop at the top of the wreath and stitch or glue in place.

As winter draws to a close, the promise of all the spring colors to come is always a welcome thought—and this garland allows you to bring a little of those spring brights into your home.

spring flower garland

MATERIALS:

DMC Natura Just Cotton (100% cotton, approx. 170yds/155m per 1¾oz/50g ball) fingering (4 ply) weight yarn
  1 ball each of shades:
    Golden Lemon N43 (A)
    Gerbera N98 (B)
    Tournesol N16 (C)
    Ivory N02 (D)
    Pistache N13 (E)

US size B/1–C/2 (2.5mm) crochet hook

Yarn needle

3 lengths of 2oz (50g) raffia

Florist's wire

Approx. 56in (140cm) length of wired artificial ivy

Pins

Needle and thread

Thin string for hanging loops

FINISHED MEASUREMENTS:

Primrose: approx. 1¼in (3cm)

Garland: approx. 60in (150cm) long

GAUGE (TENSION):

15 sts x 15 rows = 2⅜ x 2½in (6 x 6.5cm) working single crochet, using a US size B/1–C/2 (2.5mm) crochet hook.

ABBREVIATIONS:

See page 127.

SPECIAL ABBREVIATION:

make petal: *yoh, insert hook in st, yoh and pull through st, yoh and pull through 2 loops on hook; rep from * 2 more times in same st, yoh, pull through all 4 loops on hook

FOR THE GARLAND

PRIMROSE (make 22 with A center and C petals, 18 with C center and A petals, 13 with C center and B petals)

Round 1: Using either A or C, make a magic ring, 5sc into the ring.
Work in a continuous spiral, do not join.

Round 2: 2sc in each st to end, join with a sl st in first st. *10 sts.*
Fasten off.

Round 3: Join in A, B or C with a sl st, *ch3, make petal in same st as sl st, make petal in next st, ch2, sl st in same st, sl st in next st; rep from * 4 times around center (5 petals), ending last petal with sl st in base of first petal.
Fasten off.

TIP
||||||||||||||||||||||||||||||||||||||||||||||||||||||||||||

With its raffia base, this garland can be made
to any length you require—and can be
shaped to form one long swag or a couple
of smaller ones.

CHERRY BLOSSOM (make 20 with B center and D
petals, 20 with D center and B petals)

Round 1: Using either B or D, make a magic ring, 6sc into
the ring, join with a sl st in first st.
Fasten off.

Round 2: Join in contrast color B or D with a sl st, *2dc,
sl st in same st as dc, sl st in next st; rep from * 5 times
around center (6 petals), ending last petal with sl st in base
of first petal.
Fasten off.

LEAF (make 22)

Using E, ch9.

Round 1: 1sc in 2nd ch from hook, 1sc in next ch, 1hdc in
each of next 4 ch, 1sc, 2sc in last ch, do not turn, working
back down other side of ch, 1sc in each of next 2 ch, 1hdc
in each of next 4 ch, 1sc, 1sc in beg 1-ch.

Round 2: Ch1, sl st in each st to top of leaf, ch2 at top of
leaf, sl st in 2nd ch from hook, sl st in each st to base of
leaf, join with a sl st in first st.
Fasten off.

MAKING UP AND FINISHING

Block each flower and leaf.

Make up the garland base with the florist's wire and raffia,
as explained on page 125. Lay your raffia base on a flat
surface and wrap the length of artificial ivy around it from
one end to the other.

Using blocking pins, position and pin your blocked flowers
and leaves where you want them to be. Stitch the flowers
and leaves securely in place by sewing them on to the
raffia using a needle and thread.

Use thin string to attach hanging loops to the back of the
garland.

This nature-themed wreath is made up of tiny toadstools and acorns, in amongst a layer of bright fall-colored beech leaves. The wreath base used is made from twigs to keep the whole effect as natural-looking as possible.

toadstool wreath

SKILL RATING: ● ● ○

MATERIALS:

Rowan Cotton Glace (100% cotton, approx. 125yds/115m per 1¾oz/50g ball) light worsted (DK) weight yarn
1 ball each of shades:
  Ochre 833 (A)
  Toffee 843 (B)
  Oyster 730 (C)
  Ecru 725 (D)
  Poppy 741 (E)
  Blood Orange 445 (F)

US size B/1–C/2 (2.5mm) crochet hook

Stitch marker

Yarn needle

Polyester toy stuffing

12in (30cm) diameter twig wreath

Pins

Hot glue gun

Ribbon for hanging loop

FINISHED MEASUREMENTS:

Large beech leaf: approx. 3in (7.5cm)

Wreath: approx. 12in (30cm) diameter

GAUGE (TENSION):

15 sts x 15 rows = 2½ x 2⅜in (6.5 x 6cm) working single crochet, using a US size B/1–C/2 (2.5mm) crochet hook

ABBREVIATIONS:

See page 127.

FOR THE WREATH

LARGE BEECH LEAF (make 7 in A, 7 in F)

Using A or F, ch13.

Round 1: Sl st in 2nd ch from hook, 1sc, 1hdc, 1dc in each of next 3 ch, 1tr in each of next 2 ch, 1dc in each of next 2 ch, 1hdc, 2sc in last ch, do not turn, working back down other side of ch, 2sc in first ch (same ch as previous 2 sc), 1hdc, 1dc in each of next 2 ch, 1tr in each of next 2 ch, 1dc in each of next 3 ch, 1hdc, 1sc, sl st in last ch, join with a sl st in first st.

Round 2: (Ch3, sl st) in each st to top of leaf, ch4, sl st in 4th ch from hook, sl st in top of leaf, (ch3, sl st) in each st to base of leaf, join with a sl st in first st.

Stalk: Ch6, sl st in each of next 6 ch, sl st in base of leaf.
Fasten off.

SMALL BEECH LEAF (make 8 in A, 8 in F)

Using A or F, ch9.

Round 1: Sl st in first ch, 1sc, 1hdc, 1dc, 1tr in each of next 2 ch, 1dc, 1hdc, 1sc in last ch, do not turn, working back down other side of ch, 1sc in next ch, 1hdc, 1dc, 1tr in each of next 2 ch, 1dc, 1hdc, 1sc, join with a sl st in first st.

Round 2: (Ch3, sl st) in each st to top of leaf, ch4, sl st in 4th ch from hook, sl st in top of leaf, (ch3, sl st) in each st to base of leaf, join with a sl st in first st.

Stalk: Ch6, sl st in each of next 6 ch, sl st in base of leaf.
Fasten off.

ACORN CUP (make 10)

Round 1: Using B, make a magic ring, 5sc into the ring.
Work in a continuous spiral. PM in last st and move up as each round is finished.

Round 2: 2sc in each st to end. *10 sts.*

Round 3: *1sc, 2sc in next st; rep from * to end. *15 sts.*

Round 4: *1sc in each of next 2 sts, 2sc in next st; rep from * to end. *20 sts.*

Round 5: *1sc in each of next 2 sts, sc2tog; rep from * to end, join with a sl st in first st. *15 sts.*
Fasten off.

ACORN (make 10)

Round 1: Using C, make a magic ring, 4sc into the ring. Work in a continuous spiral. PM in last st and move up as each round is finished.

Round 2: 2sc in each st to end. *8 sts.*

Round 3: *1sc, 2sc in next st; rep from * to end. *12 sts.*

Rounds 4 to 7: 1sc in each st to end.

Fasten off.

TOADSTOOL STALK (make 4)

Round 1: Using yarn D, make a magic ring, 5sc into the ring. Work in a continuous spiral. PM in last st and move up as each round is finished.

Round 2: 2sc in each st to end. *10 sts.*

Round 3: *1sc, 2sc in next st; rep from * to end, join with a sl st in first st. *15 sts.*

Round 4: Ch1, 1sc BLO in each st to end, join with a sl st in first st.

Rounds 5 and 6: Ch1, working in both loops as usual, 1sc in each st to end. Do not join, work in a continuous spiral as before.

Round 7: *1sc in next st, sc2tog: rep from * to end. *10 sts.*

Rounds 8 to 11: 1sc in each st to end.

Rounds 12: 2sc in each st to end, join with a sl st in first st. *20 sts.*

Round 13: Ch2 (doesn't count as a st), *1dc, 2dc in next st; rep from * to end, join with a sl st in first st. *30 sts.*

Fasten off.

TOADSTOOL TOP (make 1 in B, 3 in E)

Round 1: Using B or E, make a magic ring, 5sc into the ring. Work in a continuous spiral. PM in last st and move up as each round is finished.

Round 2: 2sc in each st to end. *10 sts.*

Round 3: 2sc in each st to end. *20 sts.*

Round 4: *1sc, 2sc in next st; rep from * to end. *30 sts.*

Rounds 5 and 6: 1sc in each st to end.

Round 7: *1sc, 2sc in next st; rep from * to end, join with a sl st in first st. *45 sts.*

Fasten off.

MAKING UP AND FINISHING

Block the beech leaves.

Stuff each acorn, then place it inside a cup and stitch in place. Fasten off.

Stuff the stalk lightly.
On the top of the toadstool, work French knots (see page 123) in D randomly across the surface.
Sew the top of the toadstool to the stalk, adding more stuffing if needed before fastening off.

Lay the wreath on a flat surface and use blocking pins to position the beech leaves, acorns and toadstools in to place. Glue firmly in place with a hot glue gun.

To finish off the wreath, add a coordinating ribbon as a hanging loop.

SKILL RATING: ● ● ○

MATERIALS:

Cascade Sunseeker (48% acrylic, 47% cotton, 5% metallic, approx. 237yds/217m per 3½oz/100g ball) light worsted (DK) weight yarn
  1 ball each of shades:
    Silver 04 (A)
    White 35 (B)
    White Swan 26 (C)

US size C/2–D/3 (3mm) crochet hook

Stitch marker

Polyester toy stuffing

2 lengths of 2oz (50g) grey raffia

Florist's wire

Needle and matching thread

Coordinating ribbon for bows

FINISHED MEASUREMENTS:

Each oak leaf: 3½in (9cm) long

Each star: 2in (5cm) from point to opposite point

Each completed acorn: 1½in (3.5cm)

Garland: approx. 43¼in (110cm) long

GAUGE (TENSION):

15 sts x 15 rows = 2¾ x 2½in (7 x 6.5cm) working single crochet, using a US size C/2–D/3 (3mm) crochet hook.

ABBREVIATIONS:

See page 127.

winter garland

There is something very special about the first winter frost; the sparkle that it brings to the smallest of things and the delicious crunch underfoot. This winter garland aims to catch all of those feelings within its silver grey oak leaves, winter acorns, and shimmering stars.

FOR THE GARLAND

OAK LEAF (make 13)

Using A, ch14.

Round 1: 1sc in 2nd ch from hook, 1sc in each of next 3 ch, 1hdc in each of next 5 ch, 1dc in each of next 3 ch, 5dc in last ch, do not turn, working back down other side of ch, 1dc in each of next 5 ch, 1hdc in each of next 4 ch, 1sc in each of last 3 ch, join with a sl st in first st.

Round 2:

Lobe 1: 2sc in first st, sl st in next st, (1sc, 1hdc, 1dc) in next st, sl st in next st.

Lobe 2: Sl st in next st, (1sc, 1hdc, 1dc) in next st, sl st in next st.

Lobe 3: Sl st in next st, (1sc, 1hdc, 2dc) in next st, sl st in next st.

Lobe 4: Sl st in next st, (1sc, 1hdc, 2dc) in next st, sl st in next st.

Lobe 5: Sl st in next st, (1sc, 1hdc, 1dc) in next st, (1dc, 1hdc, 1sc) in next st, sl st in each of next 2 sts.

Lobe 6: (Ch2, 1dc, 1hdc) in same st as sl st, (1hdc, 1sc) in next st, sl st in next st.

Lobe 7: Ch2, (1dc, 1hdc, sl st) in next st, sl st in next st.
Lobe 8: (Sl st, ch2) in next st, (1dc, 1hdc) in next st, (1hdc, 1sc) in next st, sl st in next st.
Lobe 9: (Sl st, ch1) in next st, 2hdc in next st, 1sc, sl st in next st.
Sl st in base of leaf, ch5, sl st in each of 5 ch, sl st in base of leaf.
Fasten off.

ACORN CUP (make 13)

Round 1: Using C, make a magic ring, 5sc into the ring. Work in a continuous spiral. PM in last st and move up as each round is finished.
Round 2: 2sc in each st to end. *10 sts.*
Round 3: *1sc, 2sc in next st; rep from * to end. *15 sts.*
Round 4: *1sc in each of next 2 sts, 2sc in next st; rep from * to end. *20 sts.*
Round 5: *1sc in each of next 2 sts, sc2tog: rep to end, join with a sl st in first st. *15 sts.*
Fasten off.

ACORN (make 13)

Round 1: Using B, make a magic ring, 4sc into the ring. Work in a continuous spiral. PM in last st and move up as each round is finished.
Round 2: 2sc in each st to end. *8 sts.*
Round 3: *1sc, 2sc in next st; rep from * to end. *12 sts.*
Rounds 4 to 7: 1sc in each st to end.
Fasten off.

STAR (make 6)

Round 1: Using C, make a magic ring, 5sc into the ring. Work in a continuous spiral, do not join.
Round 2: 2sc in each st to end, join with a sl st in first st. *10 sts.*
Round 3: *Ch5, sl st in 2nd ch from hook, 1sc, 1hdc, skip last ch and next st of central circle, sl st in next st; rep from * 4 times around (5 points), ending last point with sl st in base of first point.
Fasten off.

MAKING UP AND FINISHING

Stuff each acorn, then place it inside a cup and stitch in place. Fasten off.

Make the raffia base as explained on page 123. Lay your raffia base on a flat surface and use blocking pins to position your leaves, acorns, and stars where you want them to be. Stitch them all securely in place by sewing them onto the raffia using a needle and thread.

Add a bow in a coordinating ribbon at each end of the garland. Tie small string loops at the back of the garland for hanging.

Delicate snowflakes decorate this charming wreath, each with a touch of glitter to catch the light. It's worked in a neutral color palette and will add a touch of winter glamour to any décor.

winter wreath

SKILL RATING: ● ● ○

MATERIALS:

Cascade Sunseeker (48% acrylic, 47% cotton, 5% metallic, approx. 237yds/217m per 3½oz/100g ball) light worsted (DK) weight yarn
  1 ball each of shades:
    Silver 04 (A)
    White 35 (B)
    White Swan 26 (C)

US size B/1–C/2 (2.5mm) crochet hook

12in (30cm) diameter twig wreath

Silver rubbing wax

Hot glue gun

Coordinating ribbon for hanging loop

FINISHED MEASUREMENTS:

Each large snowflake: 2¼in (5.5cm) from point to opposite point

Each small snowflake: 2in (5cm) from point to opposite point

Wreath: 12in (30cm) diameter

GAUGE (TENSION):

15 sts x 15 rows = 2¾ x 2⅜in (7 x 6cm) working single crochet, using a US size B/1–C/2 (2.5mm) crochet hook.

ABBREVIATIONS:

See page 127.

FOR THE WREATH

LARGE SNOWFLAKE (make 4 in A, 3 in B, 3 in C)

Round 1: Using A, B or C, make a magic ring, 6sc into the ring. Work in a continuous spiral, do not join.

Round 2: 2sc in each st to end, join with a sl st in first st. *12 sts.*

Round 3: *Ch4, sl st in 2nd ch from hook, ch3, sl st in 3rd ch from hook, ch2, sl st in 2nd ch from hook, sl st in same ch as first sl st of rep, sl st in each of next 2 ch from 4-ch, sl st in center st at base of 4-ch, sl st in next st of center, ch2, sl st in 2nd ch from hook, sl st in center st at base of 2-ch, sl st in next st of center; rep from * 5 more times around center (6 points), ending last point with sl st in base of first point. Fasten off.

SMALL SNOWFLAKE (make 3 in A, 4 in B, 4 in C)

Round 1: Using A, B or C, make a magic ring, 6sc into the ring, join with a sl st in first st.

Round 2: *Ch4, sl st in 2nd ch from hook, ch3, sl st in 3rd ch from hook, ch2, sl st in 2nd ch from hook, sl st in same ch as first sl st of rep, sl st in each of next 2 ch from 4-ch, sl st in center st at base of 4-ch, sl st in next st of center; rep from * 5 more times around center (6 points), ending last point with sl st in base of first point. Fasten off.

MAKING UP AND FINISHING

Block the snowflakes.

Lay the wreath on a flat surface and gently rub on some of the silver rubbing wax. Using blocking pins, position the blocked snowflakes where you want them to be. Glue firmly in place with a hot glue gun.

To finish off the wreath, add a coordinating ribbon and hanging loop at the top and stitch or glue in place.

CHAPTER 2

SPECIAL OCCASIONS

This little heart garland looks perfect strung above a mirror or a chest of drawers, and can be made in any color combination to match your décor. As a finishing touch, small brass jingle bells add a beautiful musical note when caught by the breeze.

heart garland

SKILL RATING: ● ● ◦

MATERIALS:

Rowan Cotton Glace (100% cotton, approx. 125yds/115m per 1¾oz/50g ball) light worsted (DK) weight yarn
  1 ball each of shades:
    Oyster 730 (A)
    Ecru 725 (B)
    Dawn Grey 831 (C)

US size C/2–D/3 (3mm) crochet hook

Stitch marker

Polyester toy stuffing

64in (160cm) of narrow cord/ribbon

Short lengths of ribbon for heart hanging loops

10 jingle bells, 10mm size

Short lengths of ribbon for attaching the bells

FINISHED MEASUREMENTS:

Each heart: approx. 2¾ x 2¾in (7 x 7cm) at widest point

Garland: approx. 45in (114cm) long

GAUGE (TENSION):

15 sts x 15 rows = 2¾ x 2½in (7 x 6.5cm) working single crochet, using a US size C/2–D/3 (3mm) crochet hook.

ABBREVIATIONS:

See page 127.

FOR THE GARLAND

HEART (make 2 in A, 2 in B, 3 in C)

Heart lobes (make 2 for each heart)

Round 1: Using A, B or C, make a magic ring, 5sc into the ring.
Work in a continuous spiral. PM in last st and move up as each round is finished.

Round 2: 2sc in each st to end. 10 sts.

Round 3: *1sc, 2sc in next st; rep from * to end. *15 sts.*

Round 4: *1sc in each of first 2 sts, 2sc in next st; rep from * to end. *20 sts.*

Rounds 5 to 8: 1sc in each st to end.
On first lobe, join with a sl st at end of round 8 and fasten off.
On second lobe, do not join with sl st or fasten off.

Joining the lobes:

Holding second lobe, place first lobe next to it so first side is nearest to you. Flatten both lobes so four edges are together. Join two inner edges only with a sc seam, working 6sc so seam is on inside of completed heart. PM in last st of seam. This will mark the beg/end of round. Move it up as indicated on each round as you work in a continuous spiral.

Round 9: Beg from marked st, work 1sc in each st around two sides of heart (approx. 35 sts, alter st count in next round if needed).

Round 10: 1sc in each st, inc or dec as necessary to 34 sts, PM in last st.

Round 11: 1sc in each of next 6 sts, sc2tog, 1sc in each of next 16 sts, sc2tog, 1sc in each of next 8 sts. PM in last st. *32 sts.*

Round 12: 1sc in each of next 6 sts, sc2tog, 1sc in each of next 7 sts, sc2tog, 1sc in each of next 6 sts, sc2tog, 1sc in each of next 7 sts, PM in last st. *29 sts.*

Round 13: 1sc in each of next 6 sts, sc2tog, 1sc in each of next 6 sts, sc2tog, 1sc in each of next 5 sts, sc2tog, 1sc in each of next 5 sts (1 st before marker), sc2tog, PM in last st. *25 sts.*

Round 14: 1sc in each of next 5 sts, sc2tog, 1sc in each of next 5 sts, sc2tog, 1sc in each of next 4 sts, sc2tog, 1sc in each of next 4 sts, (1 st before marker), sc2tog, PM in last st. *21 sts.*

Round 15: 1sc in each of next 10 sts, sc2tog, 1sc in each of next 8 sts (1 st before marker), sc2tog. *19 sts.*
You may find it easier to work without the marker from this point onwards.
Stuff heart lobes.

TIP
||||||||||||||||||||||||||||||||||||||||||||||||||||||||||||||

The hearts are worked from the top downwards.
You'll make the curve lobes at the top in two
separate domes, and then join them in the
center and work down to the point in rounds.

Round 16: 1sc in each of next 9 sts, sc2tog, 1sc in each
of next 7 sts, sc2tog. *17 sts.*
Round 17: 1sc in each of next 3 sts, sc2tog, 1sc in each
of next 3 sts, sc2tog, 1sc in each of next 2 sts, sc2tog,
1sc in each of last 2 sts. *14 sts.*
Round 18: Sc2tog, 1sc in each of next 2 sts, sc2tog, 1sc
in each of next 2 sts, sc2tog, 1sc, sc2tog, 1sc, sc2tog.
9 sts.
Finish stuffing heart.
Round 19: 1sc, sc2tog, 1sc, sc2tog, 1sc, sc2tog, 1sc,
sc2tog.
Close rem hole with sl st, fasten off.

MAKING UP AND FINISHING

Sew in all ends.

Using a needle and matching thread, sew a ribbon hanging
loop to the top of each heart, between the two heart lobes.
Thread the hearts onto the garland ribbon/cord and stitch
in place with a needle and thread to stop them slipping
along the cord.

Add a small ribbon loop to each bell and sew one between
each heart as a finishing touch.

These little bobbly covers turn even the most ordinary of jam jars into the perfect table top decoration for a wedding—whether it's as a tea light holder, a sweet jar, or even a vase for small posies. For that additional touch, each jar can be personalized with a tag to make it extra special for the day.

wedding jars

TIPS
||||||||||||||||||||||||||||||||||||||||||||||||||||||||||

To create a neat joining seam at the back of the jar where each round joins, sl st at the end of each round, make 1 chain and work the first single crochet of the next round into the same stitch as the chain 1. Use a stitch marker to mark the chain at the beginning of the round to help you keep track.

When working bobbles in coordinating colors, join in the bobble yarn at the beginning of each bobble row. As you work, lay this yarn color along the top of the last row of stitches so that it gets worked in as you crochet along the row. When you are ready to make a bobble, bring the bobble color up from behind your work and work the bobble. To finish the bobble, work the final yarn round hook in the main color, laying the bobble color back along the top of the last row again to keep it worked in. At the end of the row fasten off the bobble yarn, leaving an end long enough to sew in.

SKILL RATING: ● ● ●

MATERIALS:
Rowan Creative Linen (50% linen, 50% cotton, approx. 218yds/200m per 3½oz/100g ball) DK (light worsted) weight yarn
  1 ball each of shades:
    Cloud 0620 (A)
    Natural 0621 (B)

US size C/2–D/3 (3mm) crochet hook

Stitch marker

Yarn needle

3¼in (8cm) tall screw-top round glass jar

5¼in (13cm) tall screw-top round glass jar

Ribbon

Luggage/parcel tag

FINISHED MEASUREMENTS:
Small jar: 3¼in (8cm) tall, 3in (7.5cm) diameter at top

Tall jar: 5¼in (13cm) tall, 3in (7.5cm) diameter at top

GAUGE (TENSION):
15 sts x 15 rows = 3¼ x 3in (8 x 7.5cm) working single crochet, using a US size C/2–D/3 (3mm) crochet hook.

ABBREVIATIONS:
See page 127.

SPECIAL ABBREVIATIONS:
MB (make bobble): *yoh, insert hook in st, yoh and pull through st, yoh, pull yarn through 2 loops on hook; rep from * 3 more times in same st, yoh, pull through all 5 loops on hook

This cover can be adapted to any size straight-sided jar simply by making the base of the cover the same size as the base of your jar—but for the pattern to work the stitch count when you begin the sides should be a multiple of 6 + 2. Once you have the correct base size, the following rounds for the sides should fit perfectly—although the final stitch counts will vary.

FOR THE JAR COVER

BASE

Round 1: Using A or B, make a magic ring, 8sc into the ring.

Work in a continuous spiral. PM in last st and move up as each round is finished.

Round 2: 2sc in each st to end. *16 sts.*

Round 3: *1sc, 2sc in next st; rep from * to end. *24 sts.*

Round 4: *1sc in each of first 2 sts, 2sc in next st; rep from * to end. *32 sts.*

Round 5: *1sc in each of first 3 sts, 2sc in next st; rep from * to end. *40 sts.*

Round 6: 1sc in each st to end.

Round 7: *1sc in each of first 4 sts, 2sc in next st; rep from * to end. *48 sts.*

Round 8: *1sc in each of first 5 sts, 2sc in next st; rep from * to end. *56 sts.*

Round 9: 1sc in each st to end, join with a sl st in first st.

Round 10: Ch1, 1sc BLO in each st to end, join with a sl st in first st.

Begin the sides:

Round 11: Ch1, 1sc in each st to end, join with a sl st in first st.

Round 12: Ch1, 1sc in each st to end, join with a sl st in first st.

Round 13 (bobble row 1): Join in A or B contrast color but work over it in main color. Using main color, ch1, 1sc in each of first 2 sts, *MB using contrast color, working final yoh of bobble using main color, 1sc in each of next 5 sts; rep from * to end, join with a sl st in first st, leave contrast color hanging loose at back ready for next bobble round.

Rounds 14 and 15: Ch1, 1sc in each st to end, join with a sl st in first st. *56 sts.*

Round 16 (bobble row 2): Join in contrast color but work over it in main color. Using main color, ch1, 1sc in each of first 6 sts, *MB using contrast color, working final yoh of bobble using main color, 1sc in each of next 5 sts; rep from * to last 2 sts, MB using contrast color, working final yoh of bobble using main color, 1sc in last st with main color, join with a sl st in first st, leave contrast color hanging loose at back ready for next bobble round.

Rounds 17 and 18: Ch1, 1sc in each st to end, join with a sl st in first st. *56 sts.*

Round 19 (bobble row 3): Join in contrast color but work over it in main color. Using main color, ch1, 1sc in each of first 3 sts, *MB using contrast color, working final yoh of bobble using main color, 1sc in each of next 5 sts; rep from * to end, ending last rep with 1sc in each of last 4 sts, join with a sl st in first st, leave contrast color hanging loose at back ready for next bobble round.

Rounds 20 and 21: Ch1, 1sc in each st to end, join with a sl st in first st. *56 sts.*

Round 22 (bobble row 4): Join in contrast color but work over it in main color. Using main color, ch1, 1sc in first st, *MB in next st using contrast color, working final yoh of bobble using main color, 1sc in each of next 5 sts; rep from * to last 7 sts, MB in next st using contrast color, working final yoh of bobble using main color, 1sc in main color in each of last 6 sts, join with a sl st in first st.

Small jar only:

Fasten off contrast color.

Tall jar only:

Rep rounds 11–19, fastening off contrast color at end of round 19.

Both jars:

Next round: Ch1, 1sc in each st to end, join with a sl st in first st. *56 sts.*

Next round: Ch1, *1sc in each of first 4 sts, sc2tog; rep from * to last 2 sts, 1sc in each of last 2 sts, join with a sl st in first st. *47 sts.*

Next round: Ch1, *1sc in each of first 3 sts, sc2tog; rep from * to last 2 sts, 1sc in each of last 2 sts, join with a sl st in first st. *38 sts.*

Next 2 rounds: Ch1, 1sc in each st to end, join with a sl st in first st.

Fasten off.

Next round: Re-join contrast color, ch2 (does not count as st), 1hdc in each st to end, join with a sl st in first st.

Border round: [Sl st, ch2, sl st] to end, join with a sl st in first st.

Fasten off.

MAKING UP AND FINISHING

Slip the cover onto the jar and add the finishing ribbon and personalized tags.

This simple wreath is something a little different to make for a new arrival. It can either be in a simple neutral color palette as here, or to match the nursery color scheme.

new baby wreath

SKILL RATING: ● ● ●

MATERIALS:

Rowan Summerlite DK (100% cotton, approx. 142yds/130m per 1¾oz/50g ball) light worsted (DK) weight yarn
 1 ball of Pink Powder 472 (A)

Rowan Summerlite 4ply (100% cotton, approx. 191yds/175m per 1¾oz/50g ball) fingering (4 ply) weight yarn
 1 ball each of shades:
  Ecru 436 (B)
  Buttermilk 421 (C)

Cascade Ultra Pima (100% cotton, approx. 218yds/200m per 3½oz/100g ball) light worsted (DK) weight yarn
 1 ball each of shades:
  Sage 3720 (D)
  White 3728 (E)

US size C/2–D/3 (3mm) and US size B/1–C/2 (2.5mm) crochet hooks

Stitch marker

2 toy safety eyes, ⅛in (3mm) diameter

Polyester toy stuffing

Needle and thread

Brown embroidery thread

Red coloring pencil

Cord for balloon strings

10in (25cm) diameter pale wicker wreath

Pins

Hot glue gun

Coordinating ribbon for hanging loop

Cardboard luggage tag

FINISHED MEASUREMENTS:

Each daisy: 1¼in (3cm) from petal tip to opposite petal tip

Baby (with blanket): 4in (10cm) tall

Each balloon: 2¾in (7cm) long

Wreath: 10in (25cm) diameter

GAUGE (TENSION):

15 sts x 15 rows = 2½in (6.5cm) square working single crochet, using a US size C/2–D/3 (3mm) crochet hook and Rowan Summerlite DK.

15 sts x 15 rows = 2⅜in (6cm) square working single crochet, using a US size B/1–C/2 (2.5mm) crochet hook and Rowan Summerlite 4ply.

15 sts x 15 rows = 2½in (6.5cm) square working single crochet, using a US size C/2–D/3 (3mm) crochet hook and Cascade Ultra Pima.

ABBREVIATIONS:

See page 127.

SPECIAL ABBREVIATIONS:

MP (make picot): ch2, sl st in 2nd ch from hook

Welcome to
the World
Little One

MAKE IT YOURS

||||||||||||||||||||||||||||||||||||||||||||||||||||||||||

Personalize the little baby with hair and
skin color to match the newborn.

FOR THE WREATH

BABY (make 1)

Round 1: Using A and US size C/2–D/3 (3mm) hook,
make a magic ring, 4sc into the ring.
Work in a continuous spiral. PM in last st and move up as
each round is finished.

Round 2: 2sc in each st to end. *8 sts.*

Round 3: *1sc, 2sc in next st; rep from * to end. *12 sts.*

Round 4: *1sc in each of next 2 sts, 2sc in next st; rep
from * to end. *16 sts.*

Round 5: *1sc in each of next 3 sts, 2sc in next st; rep
from * to end. *20 sts.*

Rounds 6 and 7: 1sc in each st to end.
Attach safety eyes approx. 3 sts apart.

Round 8: *1sc in each of next 3 sts, sc2tog; rep from * to
end. *16 sts.*

Round 9: *1sc in each of next 2 sts, sc2tog; rep from * to end. *12 sts.*
Round 10: *1sc in each of next 4 sts, sc2tog; rep from * to end. *10 sts.*
Stuff baby.
Round 11: [1sc in each of next 3 sts, sc2tog] twice. *8 sts.*
Round 12: *1sc, 2sc in next st; rep from * to end. *12 sts.*
Round 13: *1sc, 2sc in next st; rep from * to end. *18 sts.*
Round 14: 1sc in each st to end.
Round 15: *1sc in each of next 2 sts, 2sc in next st; rep from * to end. *24 sts.*
Rounds 16 to 18: 1sc in each st to end.
Round 19: *1sc in each of next 2 sts, sc2tog; rep from * to end. *18 sts.*
Round 20: 1sc in each st to end.
Round 21: *1sc in next st, sc2tog; rep from * to end. *12 sts.*
Finish stuffing.
Round 22: [Sc2tog] to end.
Fasten off, leaving a long end.

EARS (make 2)
Using A and US size C/2–D/3 (3mm) hook, ch2, sl st in 2nd ch from hook.
Fasten off.

BLANKET (make 1)
Using US size B/1–C/2 (2.5mm) hook and B, ch61.
Row 1: 1sc in 2nd ch from hook, 1sc in each ch to end. *60 sts.*
Rows 2 to 15: Ch1, 1sc in each st to end.
Fasten off.
Picot edge: *Sl st in next st, MP, sl st in next st; rep from * to end.
Fasten off.

DAISY (make 14)
Round 1: Using C and US size B/1–C/2 (2.5mm) hook, make a magic ring, 6sc into the ring, join with a sl st in first st.
Fasten off.
Round 2: Join in B with a sl st, *ch4, 1sc in 2nd ch from hook, 1sc in each of next 2 ch, sl st in same st as prev sl st, sl st in next st of center; rep from * 6 more times around center (7 petals), ending last petal with sl st in base of first petal.
Fasten off.

BALLOON (make 2 in D, 1 in E)
Round 1: Using D or E and US size C/2–D/3 (3mm) hook, make a magic ring, 6sc into the ring.
Work in a continuous spiral. PM in last st and move up as each round is finished.
Round 2: 2sc in each st to end. *12 sts.*
Round 3: *1sc, 2sc in next st; rep from * to end. *18 sts.*
Round 4: *1sc in each of next 2 sts, 2sc in next st; rep from * to end. *24 sts.*
Round 5: 1sc in each st to end.
Round 6: *1sc in each of next 3 sts, 2sc in next st; rep from * to end. *30 sts.*
Rounds 7 to 13: 1sc in each st to end.
Round 14: *1sc in each of next 3 sts, sc2tog; rep from * to end. *24 sts.*
Round 15: *1sc in each of next 2 sts, sc2tog; rep from * to end. *18 sts.*
Round 16: *1sc in next st, sc2tog; rep from * to end. *12 sts.*
Round 17: 1sc in each st to end.
Stuff balloon.
Round 18: [Sc2tog] to end. *6 sts.*
Round 19: 1sc in each st to end, join with a sl st in first st.
Round 20: Ch2 (does not count as st), 3hdc in each st around, join with a sl st in first st. *18 sts.*
Fasten off.

MAKING UP AND FINISHING

Using the long end, sew a gathering thread around the bottom of the baby to close the remaining hole. Stitch on the ears. Using a needle and the brown embroidery thread, work some small loops for the hair. Softly color the baby's cheeks with the red coloring pencil. Wrap the blanket around the baby and sew a couple of stitches to hold it in place.

Tie a short length of cord to each balloon for the balloon string.

Block the daisies.

Lay the wreath on a flat surface and use blocking pins to position the blocked daisies and balloons where you want them to be. Glue firmly in place with a hot glue gun. Glue the baby into position.

To finish off the wreath, add a hanging loop at the top and stitch or glue in place. Finally add the cardboard luggage tag with your greeting.

MATERIALS:

Rowan Kid Classic (70% wool, 22% mohair, 8% polyamide, approx. 153yds/140m per 1¾oz/50g ball) worsted (Aran) weight yarn
  1 ball of Feather 828 (A)

Rowan Cotton Cashmere (85% cotton, 15% cashmere, approx. 137yds/125m per 1¾oz/50g ball) light worsted (DK) weight yarn
  1 ball of Golden Dunes 213 (B)

Rowan Felted Tweed DK (50% merino, 25% alpaca, 25% viscose, approx. 191yds/175m per 1¾oz/50g ball) light worsted (DK) weight yarn
  1 ball of Avocado 161 (C)

US size G/6 (4mm) and US size C/2–D/3 (3mm) crochet hooks

Pins

Needle and matching thread

3 lengths of 2oz (50g) raffia

Florist's wire

Approx. 56in (140cm) length of wired artificial ivy

Coordinating ribbon for end bows

FINISHED MEASUREMENTS:

Each large leaf: 3in (7.5cm) long

Each small leaf: 2in (5cm) long

Each rose: 2in (5cm) wide

Each rose bud: 1¼in (3cm) wide

Garland: approx. 48in (122cm) long

GAUGE (TENSION):

15 sts x 15 rows = 3 x 2¾in (7.5 x 7cm) working single crochet, using a US size G/6 (4mm) crochet hook and Rowan Kid Classic.

15 sts x 15 rows = 2¾ x 3in (7 x 7.5cm) working single crochet, using a US size C/2–D/3 (3mm) crochet hook and Rowan Cotton Cashmere.

15 sts x 15 rows = 2¾ x 2½in (7 x 6.5cm) working single crochet, using a US size C/2–D/3 (3mm) crochet hook and Rowan Felted Tweed.

ABBREVIATIONS:

See page 127.

This beautiful and classic garland will add the most personal of touches to any wedding. It's adorned with roses, rose buds, and two different-sized leaves, with extra greenery incorporated by adding a length of artificial ivy.

wedding garland

FOR THE GARLAND

ROSE (make 11 in A, 9 in B)
Using US size G/6 (4mm) hook and A or US size C/2–D/3 (3mm) hook and B, ch25.
Row 1: 1sc in 2nd ch from hook, 1sc in each ch to end. *24 sts.*
Row 2: Ch1 (does not count as st throughout), 1hdc in each st to end. *24 sts.*
Row 3: Ch1, 4sc in each of next 7 sts, 4hdc in each of next 8 sts, 4dc in each of next 9 sts. *96 sts.*
Fasten off.

ROSE BUD (make 9 in A, 11 in B)
Using US size G/6 (4mm) hook and A or US size C/2–D/3 (3mm) hook and B, ch21.
Row 1: 1sc in 2nd ch from hook, 1sc in each ch to end. *20 sts.*
Row 2: Ch1 (does not count as st throughout), 1hdc in each st to end. *20 sts.*
Row 3: Ch1, (1sc, 1hdc) in next st, (1hdc, 1sc) in next st, sl st in next st, (1sc, 1hdc, 1dc) in next st, (1dc, 1hdc, 1sc) in next st, sl st in each of next 2 sts, (1sc, 1hdc) in next st, (1hdc, 1sc) in next st, sl st in each of next 2 sts, (1hdc, 1dc) in next st, (1dc, 1hdc) in next st, sl st in each of next 2 sts, (1hdc, 1dc) in next st, (1dc, 1tr) in next st, (1tr, 1dc) in next st, (1dc, 1hdc, 1sc) in next st, sl st in last st.
Fasten off.

The roses can be made in yarn to match
the color scheme of the wedding, or add
flowers like those in the bride's bouquet
by using one of the other flower patterns.

LARGE LEAF (make 13)

Using US size C/2–D/3 (3mm) hook and C, ch13.

Round 1: 1sc in each of first 2 ch, 1hdc in each of next
2 ch, 1dc in each of next 2 ch, 1tr in each of next 3 ch,
1dc in each of next 2 ch, 1hdc in next ch, 3sc in last ch,
do not turn, working back down other side of ch, 1hdc in
next ch, 1dc in each of next 2 ch, 1tr in each of next 3 ch,
1dc in each of next 2 ch, 1hdc in each of next 2 ch, 1sc in
each of next 2 ch, join with a sl st in first st.

Round 2: Ch1, (sl st, ch2) in each st around leaf, join with
a sl st in first st.

For stalk, ch5, sl st in each of next 5 ch, sl st in base
of leaf.

Fasten off.

SMALL LEAF (make 13)

Using US size C/2–D/3 (3mm) hook and C, ch9.

Round 1: 1sc in first ch, 1hdc in each of next 2 ch, 1dc in
each of next 3 ch, 1hdc in next ch, 1sc in next ch, 3sc in
last ch, do not turn, working back down other side of ch,
1sc in next ch, 1hdc in next ch, 1dc in each of next 3 ch,
1hdc in each of next 2 ch, 1sc in last ch, sl st in first st
to join.

For stalk, ch3, sl st in each of next 3 ch, sl st in base
of leaf.

Fasten off.

MAKING UP AND FINISHING

For both the roses and the rose buds, roll the strip up to
create the shape that you want, pin in place to hold and
then stitch securely with a needle and thread.

Block each leaf.

Lay your raffia base on a flat surface and wrap the length
of artificial ivy around it from one end to the other. Using
blocking pins, position your blocked leaves and roses
where you want them to be. Stitch the flowers and leaves
securely in place by sewing them on to the raffia using a
needle and thread.

Add coordinating bows at each end of the garland and
stitch in place.

This fun, heart-shaped wreath is designed to be hung at a wedding venue and is adorned with simple flowers and a sprinkling of pink heart confetti. The color of the flowers can be co-ordinated with the wedding colors—and this can be teamed with the candle holders on page 68 to add a wonderful hand-crafted touch to any couple's special day.

wedding wreath

SKILL RATING: ● ● ○

MATERIALS:

Rowan Summerlite DK (100% cotton, approx. 142yds/130m per 1¾oz/50g ball) light worsted (DK) weight yarn
1 ball each of shades:
   Pink Powder 472 (A)
   Seashell 466 (B)
   Linen 460 (C)
   Pear 463 (D)

US size B/1–C/2 (2.5mm) crochet hook

16in (40cm) wide heart-shaped wicker wreath

Pins

Sewing needle and matching thread

Hot glue gun

Coordinating ribbon for hanging loop

FINISHED MEASUREMENTS:

Each large flower: 2¼in (5.5cm) wide

Each small flower: 1½in (4cm) wide

Each leaf: 2in (5cm) long

Each heart: 1⅜in (3.5cm) tall

Wreath: 16in (40cm) wide

GAUGE (TENSION):

15 sts x 15 rows = 2⅜in (6cm) square working single crochet, using a US size B/1–C/2 (2.5mm) crochet hook.

ABBREVIATIONS:

See page 127.

FOR THE WREATH

HEART (make 17)

Using A, ch14.

Round 1: 3sc in 2nd ch from hook, 1sc in each of next 6 ch, ch2, 1sc in each of next 6 ch, do not turn, working back down other side of ch, 3sc in first ch, 2sc in next ch, 1sc in each of next 3 ch, skip 1 ch, sl st in next ch, skip 1 ch, 1sc in each of next 3 ch, 2sc in next ch, skip last ch, join with a sl st in first st.
Fasten off.

LARGE FLOWER (make 3 with C center and B petals, 4 with B center and C petals)

Using C or B, ch29.

Row 1: 1dc in 2nd ch from hook, 1dc in each ch to end. *28 sts.*

Row 2: Ch1, 1sc in each st to end, do not turn.
Fasten off.

Row 3: Join in B or C with a sl st in first st of row 2, *(ch2, 1dc, 1tr, 1dtr) in same st as sl st, (1dtr, 1tr, 1dc, ch2, sl st) in next st, sl st in next st; rep from * 5 more times (6 petals), leave rem sts unworked.
Fasten off.

SMALL FLOWER (make 10 with C center and B petals, make 8 with B center and C petals)

Using C or B, ch21.

Row 1: 1dc in 2nd ch from hook, 1dc in each ch to end. *20 sts.*

Row 2: Ch1, 1sc in each st to end, do not turn.
Fasten off.

Row 3: Join in B or C with a sl st in first st of row 2, *(ch2, 1dc, 1tr) in same st as sl st, (1tr, 1dc, ch2, sl st) in next st, sl st in next st; rep from * 4 more times (5 petals), leave rem sts unworked.
Fasten off.

LEAF (make 14)

Using D, ch10.

Round 1: 1sc in 2nd ch from hook, 1sc in next ch, 1hdc in each of next 2 ch, 1dc in each of next 2 ch, 1hdc in each of next 2 ch, 2sc in last ch, do not turn, working back down other side of ch, 1sc in first ch, 1hdc in each of next 2 ch, 1dc in each of next 2 ch, 1hdc in each of next 2 ch, 1sc in next ch, ch1 across bottom, join with a sl st in first st.

Round 2: Ch1, 1sc in each st to top of leaf, ch3, sl st in 3rd ch from hook, sl st in same st as prev sc, 1sc in each st to end, join with a sl st in first st.
Fasten off.

MAKING UP AND FINISHING

Fold each heart in half lengthways from top to bottom and oversew a couple of stitches at the indent to pull the two heart tops together.

For both the large and small flowers, starting at the end where there are no petals, roll up the strip so that the RS of the petals is facing upwards. Pin to hold and stitch securely with a needle and thread.

Block the leaves.

Lay the wreath on a flat surface and use blocking pins to position the flowers, leaves and hearts where you want them to be. Glue firmly in place with a hot glue gun.

To finish off the wreath, add a hanging loop at the top and stitch or glue in place.

This little heart has been designed to be small and light enough to be popped in the post to a friend or loved one. Whether it's to send a message of love or thanks, or simply to let them know you are thinking about them, it cannot fail to light up someone's day.

greetings heart

SKILL RATING: ● ● ●

MATERIALS:

Rowan Cotton Glace (100% cotton, approx. 125yds/115m per 1¾oz/50g ball) light worsted (DK) weight yarn
   1 ball each of shades:
      Shell 845 (A)
      Ecru 725 (B)
      Dawn Grey 831 (C)

US size B/1 (2mm) crochet hook

6in (15cm) wide heart-shaped twig wreath

Pins

Hot glue gun

Coordinating ribbon for hanging loop

Cardboard luggage tag

FINISHED MEASUREMENTS:

Each flower: 1¼in (3cm) from petal to opposite petal

Wreath: 6in (15cm) diameter

GAUGE (TENSION):

15 sts x 15 rows = 2¼in (5.5cm) square working single crochet, using a US size B/1 (2mm) crochet hook.

ABBREVIATIONS:

See page 127.

FOR THE WREATH

FLOWER (make 6 with petals in A, 6 with petals in C)

Round 1: Using B, make a magic ring, 6sc into the ring, join with a sl st in first st.
Fasten off.

Round 2: Join in A or C with a sl st, *ch4, 1sc in 2nd ch from hook, 1sc in each of next 2 ch, sl st in same st as prev sl st, sl st in next st of center; rep from * 5 more times around center (6 petals), ending last petal with sl st in base of first petal.
Fasten off.

MAKING UP AND FINISHING

Block each flower.

Lay your twig heart on a flat surface and use blocking pins to position your flowers where you want them to be. Glue firmly in place with a hot glue gun.

To finish off the wreath, add a hanging loop at the top and stitch or glue in place. Finally add the cardboard luggage tag with your greeting.

What could be lovelier than receiving this pretty wreath when you have recently moved and are surrounded by packing boxes, wondering where on earth to start! It's small and light enough to be popped in the post and you can add a personal message on a luggage tag.

new home wreath

FOR THE WREATH

DOOR (make 2)
Using C, ch19.
Row 1: 1sc in 2nd ch from hook, 1sc in each ch to end. *18 sts.*
Rows 2 to 25: Ch1, 1sc in each st to end.
Fasten off.

BOX TREE (make 2)
Round 1: Using B, make a magic ring, 6sc into the ring.
Work in a continuous spiral. PM in last st and move up as each round is finished.
Round 2: 2sc in each st to end. *12 sts.*
Round 3: *1sc in next st, 2sc in next st; rep from * to end. *18 sts.*
Round 4: *1sc in each of next 2 sts, 2sc in next st; rep from * to end. *24 sts.*
Rounds 5 to 9: 1sc in each st to end.
Round 10: *1sc in each of next 2 sts, sc2tog; rep from * to end. *18 sts.*
Round 11: *1sc in next st, sc2tog; rep from * to end. *12 sts.*
Stuff trees.
Round 12: 1sc in each st to end.
Round 13: [Sc2tog] around.
Fasten off.

SKILL RATING: ● ● ●

MATERIALS:
Debbie Bliss Baby Cashmerino (55% wool, 33% acrylic, 12% cashmere, approx. 137yds/125m per 1¾oz/50g ball) sport (5 ply) weight yarn
　1 ball each of shades:
　　Camel 102 (A)
　　Wasabi 313 (B)
　　Citrus 018 (C)
　　Mustard 316 (D)
US size C/2–D/3 (3mm) crochet hook

Stitch marker

Polyester toy stuffing

Stiff cardboard to strengthen door

10cm (25cm) diameter light wicker wreath

Pins

Hot glue gun

2 thin sticks/straight twigs, each approx. 3¼in (8cm) long

2 coins/buttons to weight bottom of pots

String for bunting

Florist's wire

Coordinating ribbon for hanging loop

Cardboard luggage tag

FINISHED MEASUREMENTS:
Door: 3¼in (8cm) wide x 4in (10cm) tall

Each box tree: 3½in (9cm) tall

Each flag: 1¼in (3cm) long

Each ivy leaf: 2in (5cm)

Wreath: 10in (25cm) diameter

GAUGE (TENSION):
15 sts x 15 rows = 2⅜in (6cm) square working single crochet, using a US size C/2–D/3 (3mm) crochet hook.

ABBREVIATIONS:
See page 127.

POT (make 2)

Round 1: Using D, make a magic ring, 6sc into the ring. Work in a continuous spiral. PM in last st and move up as each round is finished.

Round 2: 2sc in each st to end. *12 sts.*

Round 3: *1sc in next st, 2sc in next st; rep from * to end, join with a sl st in first st. *18 sts.*

Round 4: Ch1, 1sc BLO in each st to end, join with a sl st in first st.

Round 5: Ch1, working in both loops as normal, 1sc in each st to end, join with a sl st in first st.

Round 6: Ch1, *1sc in each of next 5 sts, 2sc in next st; rep from * to end, join with a sl st in first st. *21 sts.*

Rounds 7 and 8: Ch1, 1sc in each st to end, join with a sl st in first st.

Round 9: Ch1, *1sc in each of next 6 sts, 2sc in next st; rep from * to end, join with a sl st in first st. *24 sts.*

Round 10: Sl st in each st to end.

Fasten off.

IVY LEAF (make 9)

Round 1: Using B, make a magic ring, 4sc into the ring. Work in a continuous spiral. PM in last st and move up as each round is finished.

Round 2: 2sc in each st to end. *8 sc.*

Round 3: *1sc, 2sc in next st; rep from * to end, join with a sl st in first st. *12 sc.*

Point 1: Ch3, sl st in 2nd ch from hook, 1sc, sl st in next st.

Point 2: Ch4, sl st in 2nd ch from hook, 1sc, 1hdc, skip next st of center, sl st in next st.

Point 3: Ch6, sl st in 2nd ch from hook, 1sc, 1hdc, 1dc, 1tr, skip 2 sts of center, sl st in next st.

Point 4: Rep point 2.

Point 5: Rep point 1.

Stem: Sl st in next st, ch5, sl st in 2nd ch from hook, sl st in each of next 3 ch, sl st in base of 5-ch.

Fasten off.

IVY BRANCH (make 1)

Using A, work ch to approx. 20in (50cm), or desired length. Fasten off.

FLAG (make 2 in A, 1 in B and 2 in C)

Using A, B or C, ch2.

Row 1: 2sc in 2nd ch from hook.

Row 2: Ch1, 1sc in next st, 2sc in next st. *3 sts.*

Row 3: Ch1, 2sc in first st, 1sc, 2sc in last st. *5 sts.*

Row 4: Ch1, 1 sc in each st to end.

Edging: Ch1, 1sc in each row end to bottom of flag, ch1 over point at bottom of flag, 1sc in each row end up other side of flag, join with a sl st in first st.

Fasten off.

MAKE IT YOURS

Personalize the door by making it in the correct color with the right house number for the new home!

MAKING UP AND FINISHING

Block the two door pieces, the ivy leaves and the flags.

Work topstitching in A to create 2 panels on one door piece. Embroider the letterbox and house number in D. Add a French knot (see page 123) as the doorknob, using two strands of D held together. Place the two door panels WS together and work a single crochet seam all around the edge to join, working a ch1 at each corner. Before joining the final side, slip a piece of stiff cardboard, cut to the right size, in between the two layers. Finish joining the last side and fasten off.

Carefully insert a short stick/twig into the center of each box tree ball. Drop a coin or button into the bottom of each pot, securing it with a dot of glue from the glue gun. Position the tree in the center of the pot and fill the pot with glue from the hot glue gun. Hold the tree in place just whilst the glue sets to avoid it moving.

Lay the wreath on a flat surface and wrap around the ivy branch in the position you want it to be. Pin in place to hold and then use the hot glue gun to secure it firmly. Use blocking pins to position the ivy leaves then stick in place with the glue gun.

Tie a piece of string from one side of the wreath to the other and stick the flags onto the string with the glue gun.

Carefully thread some double thickness florist's wire across the back of each pot and then wire the pot to the wreath securely.

To attach the door to the wreath, carefully thread some double thickness florist's wire across the WS at the bottom of the door and then wire the door to the wreath securely.

To finish off the wreath, add a hanging loop at the top and stitch or glue in place. Finally, add the cardboard luggage tag with your greeting.

Candles are the perfect romantic touch to a wedding venue and they'll look even more special in these simple ring holders. You can make them to match the heart-shaped wedding wreath on page 59 for a coordinated look.

wedding candle rings

on page 59 for a coordinated look.

SKILL RATING: ● ● ○

MATERIALS:

Rowan Summerlite DK (100% cotton, approx. 142yds/130m per 1¾oz/50g ball) light worsted (DK) weight yarn
  1 ball each of shades:
    Pink Powder 472 (A)
    Seashell 466 (B)
    Linen 460 (C)
    Pear 463 (D)

US size B/1–C/2 (2.5mm) crochet hook

Stitch marker

2 light wicker rings, each 6in (15cm) diameter

Hot glue gun

2 round candles to fit inside wicker rings

FINISHED MEASUREMENTS:

Each flower: 1in (2.5cm) diameter

Each leaf: ¾in (2cm)

Each heart: 1in (2.5cm)

Ring: 6in (15cm) diameter

GAUGE (TENSION):

15 sts x 15 rows = 2⅜in (6cm) square working single crochet, using a US size B/1–C/2 (2.5mm) crochet hook.

ABBREVIATIONS:

See page 127.

Caution: Never leave a lit candle unattended and always extinguish after use.

FOR THE RING

FLOWERS (make 12 with C center and B petals, 12 with B center and C petals)

Round 1: Using B or C, make a magic ring, 5sc into the ring, sl st in beg to join.
Fasten off.

Round 2: Join in C or B with a sl st, *(1hdc, 1dc, 1hdc, sl st) in same st as prev sl st, sl st in next st; rep from * 4 more times around center (5 petals), ending last petal with sl st in base of first petal.
Fasten off.

LEAVES (make 16)

Using D, ch6.

Round 1: Sl st in 2nd ch from hook, 1sc in next ch, 1hdc in next ch, 1sc in each of next 2 ch, ch1, do not turn, working back down other side of ch, 1sc in each of next 2 ch, 1hdc in next ch, 1sc in next ch, sl st in next ch, ch1, join with a sl st in first st.
Fasten off.

HEARTS (make 10)

Using A, ch10.

Round 1: 2sc in 2nd ch from the hook, 1sc in each of next 3 ch, (1sc, ch2, 1sc) in next ch to create V at base, 1sc in each of next 3 ch, 2sc in next ch, do not turn, working back along other side of ch, 2sc in next ch, 1sc in next ch, skip 1 ch, sl st in next ch, skip 1 ch, 1sc in next ch, 2sc in next ch, skip last ch, join with a sl st in first st.
Fasten off.

MAKING UP AND FINISHING

Block the leaves, hearts and flowers.

Fold each heart in half lengthways from top to bottom and oversew at the indent to pull the two heart tops together.

Lay the ring on a flat surface and use blocking pins to position the leaves, hearts and flowers where you want them to be. Glue firmly in place with a hot glue gun.

Add a candle inside each ring.

Small enough to post and much more fun than a shop-bought card, this wreath is decorated with balloons so it's suitable for many occasions. Personalize it with your own message on the tag.

birthday wreath

SKILL RATING: ● ● ●

MATERIALS:

DMC Petra 3 (100% cotton, approx. 306yds/280m per 3½oz/100g ball) crochet thread
1 ball each of shades:
53326 (A)
54460 (B)
5415 (C)
53045 (D)

US size B/1–C/2 (2.5mm) crochet hook

Stitch marker

Polyester toy stuffing

Cord for balloon strings

6in (15cm) diameter light wicker wreath

Pins

Hot glue gun

Coordinating ribbon for hanging loop

Cardboard luggage tag

FINISHED MEASUREMENTS:

Each balloon: 1⅜in (3.5cm) long

Wreath: 6in (15cm) diameter

GAUGE (TENSION):

15 sts x 15 rows = 2in (5cm) square working single crochet, using a US size B/1–C/2 (2.5mm) crochet hook.

ABBREVIATIONS:

See page 127.

FOR THE WREATH

BALLOON (make 3 in A, 3 in B, 3 in C and 4 in D)

Round 1: Using A, B, C or D, make a magic ring, 4sc into the ring. Work in a continuous spiral. PM in last st and move up as each round is finished.
Round 2: 2sc in each st to end. *8 sts.*
Round 3: *1sc, 2sc in next st; rep from * to end. *12 sts.*
Round 4: *1sc in each of next 2 sts, 2sc in next st; rep from * to end. *16 sts.*
Rounds 5 to 8: 1sc in each st to end.
Round 9: *1sc in each of next 2 sts, sc2tog; rep from * to end. *12 sts.*
Round 10: *1sc in next st, sc2tog; rep from * to end. *8 sts.*
Stuff balloon.
Round 11: [Sc2tog] around. *4 sts.*
Round 12: 3sc in each st around, sl st in beg to join. *12 sts.*
Fasten off.

MAKING UP AND FINISHING

Tie a short length of cord onto each balloon for the string.

Lay your wicker wreath on a flat surface and use blocking pins to position your balloons where you want them to be. Glue firmly in place with a hot glue gun.

To finish off the wreath, add a hanging loop at the top and stitch or glue in place. Finally, add the cardboard luggage tag with your greeting.

CHAPTER 3

ALL YEAR ROUND

Whether for a child's bedroom or as an addition to your Christmas decorations, this wreath is designed with simplicity and understatement in mind. The three different-sized stars have been added to a dark twig wreath to make them stand out for full effect. To give each star extra twinkle a strand of metallic thread has been worked in with the yarn.

wish upon a star wreath

MATERIALS:

Cascade Sunseeker (48% acrylic, 47% cotton, 5% metallic, approx. 237yds/217m per 3½oz/100g skein) light worsted (DK) weight yarn
   1 skein each of shades:
      Silver 04 (A)
      White 35 (B)

Drops Glitter Thread (765yds/700m per ⅜oz/10g spool) yarn
   1 spool of Silver 02 (C)

US size B/1 (2mm) crochet hook

Stitch marker

12in (30cm) diameter twig wreath

Pins

Hot glue gun

Coordinating ribbon

FINISHED MEASUREMENTS:

Each large star: approx. 2¼in (5.5cm) wide

Wreath: 12in (30cm) diameter

GAUGE (TENSION):

15 sts x 15 rows = 2⅜in (6cm) square working single crochet, using a US size B/1 (2mm) crochet hook.

ABBREVIATIONS:

See page 127.

FOR THE WREATH

LARGE STAR (make 2 in A, 1 in B)

Round 1: Using A or B held together with C, make a magic ring, 5sc into the ring.
Work in a continuous spiral. PM in last st and move up as each round is finished.
Round 2: 2sc in each st to end. *10 sts.*
Round 3: *1sc, 2sc in next st; rep from * 4 more times, join with a sl st in first st. *15 sts.*
Round 4: *Ch7, sl st in 2nd ch from hook, 1sc, 1hdc, 2dc in next ch, skip last 2 ch and next 2 sts of center, sl st in next st; rep from * 4 more times around (5 points), ending last point with sl st in base of first point.
Fasten off.

MEDIUM STAR (make 4 in A, 4 in B)

Round 1: Using A or B held together with C, make a magic ring, 5sc into the ring.
Work in a continuous spiral, do not join.
Round 2: 2sc in each st to end, join with a sl st in first st. *10 sts.*
Round 3: *Ch5, sl st in 2nd ch from hook, 1sc, 1hdc, skip last ch and next st of center, sl st in next st; rep from * 4 more times around (5 points), ending last point with sl st in base of first point.
Fasten off.

SMALL STAR (make 3 in A, 2 in B)

Round 1: Using A or B held together with C, make a magic ring, 5sc into the ring, join with a sl st in first st.
Round 2: *Ch4, sl st in 2nd ch from hook, 1sc, skip last ch, sl st in next st of center; rep from * 4 more times around (5 points), ending last point with sl st in base of first point.
Fasten off.

MAKING UP AND FINISHING

Block the stars.

Lay the wreath on a flat surface. Use blocking pins to position the blocked stars where you want them to be. Glue firmly in place with a hot glue gun.
To finish off the wreath, add a bow in a coordinating color by attaching it with a glue gun.

TIP

To give your wreath a more festive feel, use a red glitter yarn such as Cascade Sunseeker in Cherry 42 to make the stars.

Wishing on a star....

Hanging up a string of bunting instantly brightens up a child's bedroom or playroom—and this design has lots of added texture and detail, with bobbly flags and coordinating crochet beads.

bobble bunting

SKILL RATING: ● ● ○

MATERIALS:

Debbie Bliss Baby Cashmerino (55% wool, 33% acrylic, 12% cashmere, approx. 137yds/125m per 1¾oz/50g ball) sport (5 ply) weight yarn

    2 balls each of shades:
        Duck Egg 026 (A)
        Acid Yellow 091 (B)

    1 ball of shade White 100 (C)

US size C/2–D/3 (3mm) crochet hook

Yarn needle

Stitch marker

Approx. 2yds (2m) of narrow cord/ribbon

Polyester toy stuffing

2 short lengths of coordinating ribbon

FINISHED MEASUREMENTS:

Each flag: 7¼in (18cm) along top, 6¼in (16cm) from top to point

Bunting: approx. 65in (165cm) long

GAUGE (TENSION)

15 sts x 15 rows = 2½ x 2⅜in (6.5 x 6cm) working single crochet, using a US size C/2–D/3 (3mm) crochet hook.

ABBREVIATIONS:

See page 127.

SPECIAL ABBREVIATIONS:

MB (make bobble): *yoh, insert hook in st, yoh and pull through st, yoh, pull yarn through 2 loops on hook; rep from * 3 more times in same st, yoh, pull through all 5 loops on hook

FOR THE BUNTING

FLAG (make 3)

Using A, ch2.

Row 1: 3sc in 2nd ch from hook. *3 sts.*

Row 2: Ch1, 1sc in each st to end.

Row 3: Ch1, 2sc in first st, 1sc, 2sc in last st. *5 sts.*

Row 4: Rep row 2.

Row 5: Join in B but work over it in A. Using A, ch1, 2sc in first st, 1sc, MB in next st using B and working final yoh of bobble using A, 1sc in next st, 2sc in last st, fasten off B. *7 sts.*

Row 6: Rep row 2.

Row 7: Ch1, 2sc in first st, 1sc in each st to last st, 2sc in last st. *9 sts.*

Row 8: Rep row 2.

Row 9: Join in B but work over it in A. Using A, ch1, 2sc in first st, 1sc, MB using B and working final yoh of bobble using A, 1sc in each of next 3 sts, MB, 1sc, 2sc in last st, fasten off B. *11 sts.*

Row 10: Rep row 2.

Row 11: Rep row 7. *13 sts.*

Row 12: Rep row 2.

Row 13: Join in B but work over it in A. Using A, ch1, 2sc in first st, 1sc, *MB using B and working final yoh of bobble using A, 1sc in each of next 3 sts; rep from * to last 3 sts, MB, 1sc, 2sc in last st, fasten off B. *15 sts.*

Cont as set, inc in first and last st on every other row and working a bobble row every 4th row until there are 9 rows of bobbles. *39 sts.*

Next 4 rows: Rep rows 10 and 11 twice. *43 sts.*

Fasten off A.

Make the bobble border:

Round 1: Beg at top right-hand corner and with RS facing, join in C, 1sc in each st to end, 2sc in corner st, 1sc in each row end down to tip, 3sc in st at tip, 1sc in each row end up to corner, 2sc in corner st, sl st in first sc to join. Do not fasten off.

Round 2: Ch1, turn so WS of flag is facing you, sl st in first st, *[yoh, insert hook in st then pull loop through and up to dc height] 4 times in next st, yoh, pull through all loops on hook, ch1 to secure bobble, sl st in next st; rep from * to end of round, sl st in first st to join.

Fasten off.

Make 3 more flags in B with bobbles in A.

When working bobbles in coordinating colors, join in the bobble yarn at the beginning of each bobble row. As you work, lay this yarn color along the top of the last row of stitches so that it gets worked in as you crochet along the row. When you are ready to make a bobble, bring the bobble color up from behind your work and work the bobble. To finish the bobble, work the final yarn over hook in the main color, laying the bobble color back along the top of the last row again to keep it worked in. At the end of the row fasten off the bobble yarn, leaving an end long enough to sew in.

LARGE CROCHET BEAD (make 6 in A, 6 in B)

Round 1: Using A or B, make a magic ring, 6sc into the ring.
Work in a continuous spiral. PM in last st and move up as each round is finished.
Round 2: 2sc in each st. *12 sts.*
Round 3: *1sc, 2sc in next st; rep from * to end. *18 sts.*
Round 4: *1sc in each of next 2 sts, 2sc in next st; rep from * to end. *24 sts.*
Rounds 5 and 6: 1sc in each st to end.
Round 7: *1sc in each of next 2 sts, sc2tog; rep from * to end. *18 sts.*
Round 8: *1sc, sc2tog; rep from * to end. *12 sts.*
Stuff bead firmly.
Round 9: [Sc2tog] to end. *6 sts.*
Fasten off, leaving a long end.

SMALL CROCHET BEAD (make 3 in A, 3 in B)

Round 1: Using A or B, make a magic ring, 5sc into the ring.
Work in a continuous spiral. PM in last st and move up as each round is finished.
Round 2: 2sc in each st to end. *10 sts.*
Round 3: *1sc, 2sc in next st; rep from * to end. *15 sts.*
Round 4: 1sc in each st to end.
Round 5: *1sc, sc2tog; rep from * to end. *10 sts.*
Stuff bead firmly.
Round 9: [Sc2tog] to end. *5 sts.*
Fasten off, leaving a long end.

MAKING UP AND FINISHING

On the beads, thread the long yarn end onto a yarn needle and use it to close the hole left at the bottom. Sew in all the ends on the flags and crocheted beads.

Block the flags, and then finish them by sewing an opposite color small bead at the tip of each flag. Thread each flag and the large beads onto thin white ribbon or cord, positioning two large beads between each flag, alternating colors of the beads to the flags, and placing one bead at each end of the bunting.

To finish off the bunting, add a ribbon bow in a coordinating color at each end.

There can be nothing more summery than a field of bright white daisies, and this wreath will certainly bring a breath of fresh air into any room. With the bees settling happily on the flowers, you can practically hear the buzzing! The wreath is made up of two different-sized daisies and four tiny bees.

daisy and bee wreath

FOR THE WREATH

LARGE DAISY (make 8)

Round 1: Using A, make a magic ring, 6sc into the ring. Work in a continuous spiral, do not join.

Round 2: 2sc in each st to end, join with a sl st in first st. *12 sts.* Fasten off A.

Round 3: Join in B with a sl st, *ch7, 1sc BLO in 2nd ch from hook, 1hdc BLO in each of next 5 ch, sl st in same st as prev sl st, sl st in next st of center; rep from * 10 more times around center (11 petals), sl st in base of first petal.
Fasten off.

SKILL RATING: ● ● ●

MATERIALS:

DMC Natura Just Cotton (100% cotton, approx. 169yds/155m per 1¾oz/50g ball) fingering (4 ply) weight yarn
   1 ball each of shades:
     Tournesol N16 (A)
     Ibiza N01 (B)
     Pistacho N13 (C)

US size B/1 (2mm) crochet hook

Stitch marker

Yarn needle

Thin black fiber tip pen

12in (30cm) diameter twig wreath

Hot glue gun

Ribbon for hanging loop

FINISHED MEASUREMENTS:

Large daisy: 2¼in (5.5cm) wide

Wreath: 12in (30cm) diameter

GAUGE (TENSION):

15 sts x 15 rows = 2⅜in (6cm) square working single crochet, using a US size B/1 (2mm) crochet hook

ABBREVIATIONS:

See page 127.

SMALL DAISY (make 7)

Round 1: Using A, make a magic ring, 4sc into the ring. Work in a continuous spiral, do not join.

Round 2: 2sc in each st to end, join with a sl st in first st. *8 sts.*

Fasten off A.

Round 3: Join in B with a sl st, *ch6, 1sc BLO in 2nd ch from hook, 1sc BLO in each of next 4 ch, sl st in same st as prev sl st, sl st in next st of center; rep from * 7 more times around center (8 petals), ending last petal with sl st in base of first petal.

Fasten off.

LEAF (make 12)

Using C, ch12.

Round 1: Sl st in 2nd ch from hook, 1sc in each of next 2 ch, 1hdc in each of next 2 ch, 1dc in each of next 3 ch, 1hdc in each of next 2 ch, 2sc in last ch, do not turn, working back down other side of ch, 1sc in first ch, 1hdc in each of next 2 ch, 1dc in each of next 3 ch, 1hdc in each of next 2 ch, 1sc in next ch, sl st in last ch, join with a sl st in first st.

Fasten off.

BEE BODY (make 4)

Round 1: Using A, make a magic ring, 4sc into the ring. Work in a continuous spiral. PM in last st and move up as each round is finished.

Round 2: 2sc in each st to end. *8 sts.*

Rounds 3 to 6: 1sc in each st to end. *8 sts.*

Poke any yarn ends inside bee's body, adding small pieces of scrap yarn if needed.

Round 7: [Sc2tog] to end. *4 sts.*

Fasten off.

BEE WING (make 1 per bee)

Using B, ch2.

Row 1: (1hdc, 2dc, 1hdc, sl st, 1hdc, 2dc, 1hdc, sl st) in 2nd ch from hook.

Fasten off.

MAKING UP AND FINISHING

Block the daisies and leaves.

Using a thin black fiber tip pen, dot on two eyes and add three to four thin stripes around each bee's body.
Fold the wings in half to make the wing shape and sew one to each bee's back.
Sew in any ends.

Lay the wreath on a flat surface. Using blocking pins, position and pin the blocked daisies and leaves where you want them to be. Glue firmly in place with a hot glue gun. Glue the bees into position.

To finish off the wreath, add a hanging loop at the top of the wreath and stitch or glue in place.

This garland is very simple in design and works particularly well in neutral colors and tones, with the brass bells adding to the overall natural feel. The birdhouses have a front and a back piece so that, when joined together, they have a strong rigid shape.

shaker birdhouse garland

MATERIALS:

Rowan Cotton Glace (100% cotton, approx. 125yds/115m per 1¾oz/50g ball) light worsted (DK) weight yarn
  2 balls of shade Oyster 730 (A)
  1 ball each of shades:
    Ochre 833 (B)
    Mineral 856 (C)
    Ecru 725 (D)

Gold embroidery thread

Black embroidery thread

US size C/2–D/3 (3mm) and US size B/1 (2mm) crochet hooks

Stitch marker

Yarn needle

Polyester toy stuffing

String for hanging loops

13 brass bells, 10mm size

70in (175cm) of rope for the garland

14 short lengths of ribbon

FINISHED MEASUREMENTS:

Bird: approx. 3½in (9cm) from beak to tail

Birdhouse: approx. 4in (10cm) high

Garland: approx. 58in (145cm) long

GAUGE (TENSION):

15 sts x 15 rows = 2¾ x 2½in (7 x 6.5cm) working single crochet, using a US size C/2–D/3 (3mm) crochet hook.

ABBREVIATIONS:

See page 127.

FOR THE GARLAND

BIRD (make 3 in A, 4 in B)

Round 1: Using A or B and US size C/2–D/3 (3mm) hook, make a magic ring, 6sc into the ring.
Work in a continuous spiral. PM in last st and move up as each round is finished.
Round 2: 2sc in each st to end. *12 sts.*
Round 3: *1sc, 2sc in next st; rep from * to end. *18 sts.*
Rounds 4 to 6: 1sc in each st to end.
Round 7: 1sc in each of first 10 sts, 2sc in next st, 1sc in each of next 2 sts, 2sc in next st, 1sc in each of last 4 sts. *20 sts.*
Round 8: 1sc in each of first 12 sts, [2sc in next st, 1 sc in next st] 4 times. *24 sts.*
Round 9: 1sc in each st to end.
Round 10: 1sc in each of first 15 sts, [2sc in next st, 1sc in each of next 2 sts] 3 times. *27 sts.*
Round 11: 1sc in each of first 14 sts, 2sc in next st, 1sc in each of next 3 sts, 1hdc in each of next 5 sts, 1sc in each of next 3 sts, 2sc in last st. *29 sts.*
Round 12: 1sc in each of first 4 sts, sc2tog, 1sc, sc2tog, 1sc in each of next 9 sts, 2sc in next st, 1sc in each of next 2 sts, 2sc in next st, 1sc in each of last 7 sts. *29 sts.*
Round 13: 1sc in each of first 5 sts, sc2tog, 1sc in each of next 5 sts, 2sc in next st, 1sc in each of next 2 sts, 2sc in next st, 1sc in each of next 3 sts, 1hdc, 1sc in each of next 2 sts, 2sc in next st, 1sc in each of last 6 sts. *31 sts.*
Round 14: 1sc in each of first 5 sts, [sc2tog] twice, 1sc in each of next 10 sts, 1hdc in each of next 6 sts, 1sc in each of last 6 sts. *29 sts.*
Round 15: 1sc in each of first 4 sts, [sc2tog] twice, 1sc, sc2tog, 1sc in each of last 18 sts. *26 sts.*
Round 16: 1sc in each of first 2 sts, [sc2tog] 4 times, 1sc in each of next 5 sts, 1hdc in each of next 8 sts, 1sc in each of next 3 sts. *22 sts.*
Round 17: 1sc in each of first 3 sts, [sc2tog] twice and stop. Join 2 sides tog along bottom of bird with a sc seam, working 6sc.
Lightly stuff head and bottom curve of body.
Make the tail:
Flatten end of bird, join in A or B contrast color, ch1, 4sc evenly across tail end, turn.
Row 1: Ch1, 2sc in first st, 1sc in each of next 2 sts, 2sc in last st, turn. *6 sts.*
Row 2: Ch1, sl st in first st, skip next st, (2hdc, 2dc) in next st, (2dc, 2hdc) in next st, skip next st, sl st in last st.
Fasten off.

WING 1 (make 4 in A, 3 in B)

Using contrast yarn to body and US size C/2–D/3 (3mm) hook, ch8.

Row 1: 1sc in 2nd ch from hook, 1sc in next ch, 1hdc in each of next 2 ch, 1dc in each of next 2 ch, (3dc, 1sc) in last ch, do not turn, working back down other side of ch, 1sc in each of next 5 ch, sl st in last st, join with a sl st in first st.

Fasten off.

WING 2 (make 4 in A, 3 in B)

Using contrast yarn to body and US size C/2–D/3 (3mm) hook, ch7.

Row 1: 1sc in 2nd ch from hook, 1sc in each of next 5 ch, do not turn, working back down other side of ch, 4dc in same ch as last sc, 1dc in next st, 1hdc in each of next 2 sts, 1sc in each of last 2 sts, join with a sl st in first st.

Fasten off.

BEAK (make 7)

Using gold embroidery thread and US size B/1 (2mm) hook, ch2.

Row 1: 2sc in 2nd ch from hook. *2 sts.*

Row 2: Ch1, 1sc in first st, 2sc in last st. *3 sts.*

Row 3: Ch1, 2sc in first st, 1sc, 2sc in last st. *5 sts.*

Row 4: Ch1, 2sc in first st, 1sc in each of next 3 sts, 2sc in last st. *7 sts.*

Fasten off, leaving long tail.

BIRDHOUSE (make 3 in A, 3 in D)

Make a front and back for each house.

Using A or D and US size C/2–D/3 (3mm) hook, ch11.

Row 1: 1sc in 2nd ch from hook, 1sc each of next 9 ch. *10 sts.*

Row 2: Ch1, 1sc in each st to end.

Row 3: Ch1, 2sc in first st, 1sc in each st to last st, 2sc in last st. *12 sts.*

Row 4: Ch1, 1sc in each st to end.

Row 5: Rep row 3. *14 sts.*

Row 6: Rep row 4.

Row 7: Rep row 3. *16 sts.*

Rows 8 to 10: Ch1, 1sc in each st to end.

Row 11: Rep row 3. *18 sts.*

Row 12: Rep row 4.

Rows 13 to 20: Ch1, [sc2tog] to end. *2 sts.*

Row 21: Sc2tog.

Fasten off.

To make the roof:

Row 1: Using B or C, ch4, rejoin yarn on top right-hand side of house. Work 10sc up side to top point, 2sc in each of top 2 sts, 10sc down other side, ch4, turn.

Row 2: Sl st in first st, 1sc in each st to top point of roof, 2sc in each of top 2 sts, 1sc in each st down other side of roof, sl st in last st, turn.

Row 3: Sl st in first st, 1sc in each st to top point of roof, 2sc in each of top 2 sts, 1sc in each st down other side of roof, sl st in last st.

Fasten off.

TIP
IIIIIIIIIIIIIIIIIIIIIIIIIIIIIIIIIIIIIIIIIIIIIIIIIIIIIII

To neaten the join between the house and the roof you can work a top stitch (sl st through the house from top to bottom) along the line where the roof and the house meet.

Join front and back of house:
With front and back pieces WS tog, starting at bottom right of roof and working through both pieces to join, re-join yarn to match roof and work sc up right side of roof, 2sc in top st, ch3, sl st in 3rd ch from hook, work sc down other side of roof, sl st in last st.
Fasten off.
Re-join yarn to match house just below roof. Working through both pieces, sc around sides and bottom of house.
Fasten off.

DOOR (make 1 per house to match roof)
Round 1: Using US size C/2–D/3 (3mm) hook, make a magic ring, 6sc into the ring.
Work in a continuous spiral. PM in last st and move up as each round is finished.
Round 2: 2sc in each st to end. *12 sts.*
Round 3: *1sc, 2sc in next st; rep from * to end. *18 sts.*
Round 4: *1sc in each of first 2 sts, 2sc in next st; rep from * to end. *24 sts.*
Round 5: Sl st in each st to end.
Fasten off.

MAKING UP AND FINISHING
To finish each bird, sew a wing on each side with the pointed end toward the front. Embroider eyes with the black embroidery thread.
Use the long tail to secure the beak shape, and then to sew the beak onto the bird.

Thread a bell onto the middle of a length of string, and knot just above it. Thread both ends of the string up through the bird, from the bottom of the tummy to the middle back of the neck, and tie each bird onto the hanging rope.

Thread another length of string through the top point of each birdhouse and use it to tie the birdhouse onto the rope between each pair of birds.

Stitch a door onto the front of each house. Use a length of string to add a hanging loop at the top of each house, adding the bell at the same time.

To finish, tie a short length of ribbon between each item.

This pretty garland, with its vivid oranges, pinks, and reds, will brighten up any room for a shot of instant summer color. It's made up of both large and small Gerberas, worked in three different colors.

gerbera garland

SKILL RATING: ● ● ●

MATERIALS:

Katia Merino Baby (100% virgin wool, approx. 180yds/165m per 1¾oz/50g ball) sport (5 ply) weight yarn

1 ball each of shades:
56 (A)
60 (B)
04 (C)
49 (D)

US size B/1–C/2 (2.5mm) crochet hook

Florist's wire

3 lengths of 2oz (50g) raffia

Pins

Coordinating ribbon

Needle and matching thread

FINISHED MEASUREMENTS:

Large gerbera: approx. 2½in (6.5cm) wide

Small gerbera: 2in (5cm) wide

Garland: approx. 58in (147cm) long

GAUGE (TENSION):

15 sts x 15 rows = 2in (5cm) square working single crochet, using a US size B/1–C/2 (2.5mm) crochet hook.

ABBREVIATIONS:

See page 127.

FOR THE GARLAND

LARGE GERBERA (make 8 in B, 7 in C, 6 in D)

Round 1: Using A, make a magic ring, 6sc into the ring.
Work in a continuous spiral, do not join.
Round 2: 2sc in each st to end, join with a sl st in first st. *12 sts.*
Fasten off A.
Round 3: Join in B, C or D with a sl st, *ch8, 1sc in 2nd ch from hook, 1hdc in next ch, 1dc in each of next 4 ch, 1hdc in last ch, sl st in next st of center; rep from * 10 more times around center (11 petals), sl st in base of first petal.
Fasten off.

SMALL GERBERA (make 8 in B, 7 in C, 7 in D)

Round 1: Using A, make a magic ring, 4sc into the ring.
Work in a continuous spiral, do not join.
Round 2: 2sc in each st to end, join with a sl st in first st. *8 sts.*
Fasten off.
Round 3: Join in B, C or D with a sl st, *ch7, 1sc in 2nd ch from hook, 1hdc in each of next 4 ch, 1sc in last ch, sl st in next st of center; rep from * 7 more times around center (8 petals), ending last petal with sl st in base of first petal.
Fasten off.

MAKING UP AND FINISHING

Block the flowers.

Make up the garland base with the florist's wire and raffia, as explained on page 125. Lay your base on a flat surface. Using blocking pins, position and pin your blocked flowers where you want them to be. Stitch the flowers securely in place by sewing them onto the raffia using a needle and thread.

To finish off the garland, add bows in a coordinating color at each end and in the center, stitching them in place with a needle and thread.

With this little bird quietly sitting on her nest full of eggs, this wreath will add a touch of spring to your home all year round. It's simple in design, with just the addition of trailing ivy leaves wrapped around a twig wreath base.

nesting birds wreath

SKILL RATING: ● ● ○

MATERIALS:

Willow and Lark Ramble (100% wool, approx. 136yds/125m per 1¾oz/50g ball) light worsted (DK) weight yarn
  1 ball each of shades:
    Feather Grey Melange 103 (A)
    Puddle Blue Melange 120 (B)
    Lichen Green 115 (C)

Willow and Lark Woodland (50% wool, 25% alpaca and 25% viscose, approx. 191yds/175m per 1¾oz/50g ball) light worsted (DK) weight yarn
  1 ball of shade Toffee 404 (D)

Gold embroidery thread

US size C/2–D/3 (3mm) and US size B/1 (2mm) crochet hooks

Polyester toy stuffing

Stitch marker

Yarn needle

Black embroidery thread

Sewing needle

12in (30cm) diameter twig wreath

Hot glue gun

Invisible nylon thread for hanging the bird

Ribbon for hanging loop and bow

FINISHED MEASUREMENTS:

Bird: approx. 3½in (9cm) from beak to tail

Wreath: approx. 12in (30cm) diameter

GAUGE (TENSION):

15 sts x 15 rows = 2⅜in (6cm) square working single crochet, using a US size C/2–D/3 (3mm) crochet hook.

ABBREVIATIONS:

See page 127.

FOR THE WREATH

BIRD (make 2, alt A and B)

Round 1: Using A or B and US size C/2–D/3 (3mm) hook, make a magic ring, 6sc into the ring.
Work in a continuous spiral. PM in last st and move up as each round is finished.
Round 2: 2sc in each st to end. *12 sts.*
Round 3: *1sc, 2sc in next st; rep from * to end. *18 sts.*
Rounds 4 to 6: 1sc in each st to end.
Round 7: 1sc in each of first 10 sts, 2sc in next st, 1sc in each of next 2 sts, 2sc in next st, 1sc in each of last 4 sts. *20 sts.*
Round 8: 1sc in each of first 12 sts, [2sc in next st, 1sc in next st] 4 times. *24 sts.*
Round 9: 1sc in each st to end.
Round 10: 1sc in each of first 15 sts, [2sc in next st, 1sc in each of next 2 sts] 3 times. *27 sts.*
Round 11: 1sc in each of first 14 sts, 2sc in next st, 1sc in each of next 3 sts, 1hdc in each of next 5 sts, 1sc in each of next 3 sts, 2sc in last st. *29 sts.*
Round 12: 1sc in each of first 4 sts, sc2tog, 1sc, sc2tog, 1sc in each of next 9 sts, 2sc in next st, 1sc in each of next 2 sts, 2sc in next st, 1sc in each of last 7 sts. *29 sts.*
Round 13: 1sc in each of first 5 sts, sc2tog, 1sc in each of next 5 sts, 2sc in next st, 1sc in each of next 2 sts, 2sc in next st, 1sc in each of next 3 sts, 1hdc, 1sc in each of next 2 sts, 2sc in next st, 1sc in each of last 6 sts. *31 sts.*
Round 14: 1sc in each of first 5 sts, [sc2tog] twice, 1sc in each of next 10 sts, 1hdc in each of next 6 sts, 1sc in each of last 6 sts. *29 sts.*
Round 15: 1sc in each of first 4 sts, [sc2tog] twice, 1sc, sc2tog, 1 sc in each of last 18 sts. *26 sts.*
Round 16: 1sc in each of first 2 sts, [sc2tog] 4 times, 1sc in each of next 5 sts, 1hdc in each of next 8 sts, 1sc in each of last 3 sts. *22 sts.*
Round 17: 1sc in each of first 3 sts, [sc2tog] twice and stop. Join 2 sides tog along bottom of bird with a sc seam, working 6sc.
Lightly stuff head and bottom curve of body.
To make the tail:
Row 1: Flatten end of bird, join in contrast color, ch1, 4sc evenly across tail end, turn.
Row 2: Ch1, 2sc in each st to end, turn. *8 sts.*
Row 3: Ch1, sl st in first st, skip next 2 sts, (1sc, 1hdc, 1dc, 1tr) in next st, (1tr, 1dc, 1hdc, 1sc) in next st, skip next 2 sts, sl st in last st.
Fasten off.

WING 1 (make 2)

Using contrast color A or B and US size C/2–D/3 (3mm) hook, ch7.

Row 1: 1sc in 2nd chain from hook, 1sc in next ch, 1hdc in each of next 2 ch, 1dc in each of next 2 ch, (3dc, 1sc) in last ch, do not turn, working back down other side of ch, 1sc in each of next 5 ch, join with a sl st in first st.
Fasten off.

WING 2 (make 2)

Using contrast color A or B and US size C/2–D/3 (3mm) hook, ch7.

Row 1: 1sc in 2nd ch from hook, 1sc in each of next 5ch, do not turn, working back down other side of ch, 4dc in same ch as last sc, 1dc, 1hdc in each of next 2 ch, 1sc in each of next 2 ch, join with a sl st in first st.
Fasten off.

BEAK (make 2)

Using gold embroidery thread and US size B/1 (2mm) hook, ch2.

Row 1: 2sc in 2nd ch from hook, turn. *2 sts.*
Row 2: Ch1, 1sc in first st, 2sc in last st, turn. *3 sts.*
Row 3: Ch1, 2sc in first st, 1sc, 2sc in last st, turn. *5 sts.*
Row 4: Ch1, 2sc in first st, 1sc in each of next 3 sts, 2sc in last st, turn. *7 sts.*
Fasten off, leaving a long tail.

NEST

Round 1: Using D and US size C/2–D/3 (3mm) hook, make a magic ring, 8sc into the ring.
Work in a continuous spiral. PM in last st and move up as each round is finished.
Round 2: 2sc in each st to end. *16 sts.*
Round 3: *1sc, 2sc in next st; rep from * to end. *24 sts.*
Round 4: *2sc, 2sc in next st; rep from * to end. *32 sts.*
Round 5: *3sc, 2sc in next st; rep from * to end. *40 sts.*
Round 6: *4sc, 2sc in next st; rep from * to end. *48 sts.*
Round 7: 1sc in each st to end.
Round 8: *5sc, 2sc in next st; rep from * to end. *56 sts.*
Rounds 9 to 17: 1sc in each st to end.
Round 18: *5sc, sc2tog; rep from * to end. *48 sts.*
Round 19: *4sc, sc2tog; rep from * to end. *40 sts.*
Fasten off.

EGG (make 6)

Round 1: Using A and US size C/2–D/3 (3mm) hook, make a magic ring, 6sc into the ring.
Work in a continuous spiral. PM in last st and move up as each round is finished.
Round 2: *1sc, 2sc in next st; rep from * to end. *9 sts.*
Round 3: *2sc, 2sc in next st; rep from * to end. *12 sts.*
Rounds 4 to 6: 1sc in each st to end.
Round 7: *1sc, sc2tog; rep from * to end. *8 sts.*
Stuff the egg.
Round 8: [Sc2tog] to end. *4 sts.*
Fasten off, using long end to gather and close hole.

LARGE IVY LEAF (make 12)

Round 1: Using C and US size C/2–D/3 (3mm) hook, make a magic ring, 5sc into the ring.
Work in a continuous spiral. PM in last st and move up as each round is finished.
Round 2: 2sc in each st to end. *10 sts.*
Round 3: *1sc, 2sc in next st; rep from * to end, join with a sl st in first st. *15 sts.*

Point 1: Ch4, sl st in 2nd ch from hook, 1sc, 1hdc, skip next st of center, sl st in next st of center.
Point 2: Ch5, sl st in 2nd ch from hook, 1sc, 1hdc, 1dc, skip next st of center, sl st in next st of center.
Point 3: Ch7, sl st in 2nd ch from hook, 1sc, 1hdc, 1dc, 1tr, 1dtr, skip next 2 sts of center, sl st in next st of center.
Point 4: Rep point 2.
Point 5: Rep point 1.
Sl st in base of leaf, ch5, sl st in each of next 5 ch, sl st in base of leaf.
Fasten off.

SMALL IVY LEAF (make 10)

Round 1: Using C and US size C/2–D/3 (3mm) hook, make a magic ring, 4sc into the ring.
Work in a continuous spiral, do not join.
Round 2: 2sc in each st to end. *8 sts.*
Round 3: *1sc, 2sc in next st; rep from * to end, sl st in first st of round to join. *12 sts.*
Point 1: Ch3, sl st in 2nd ch from hook, 1sc, sl st in next st of center.
Point 2: Ch4, sl st in 2nd ch from hook, 1sc, 1hdc, skip next st of center, sl st in next st of center.
Point 3: Ch6, sl st in 2nd ch from hook, 1sc, 1hdc, 1dc, 1tr, skip next 2 sts of center, sl st in next st of center.
Point 4: Rep point 2.
Point 5: Rep point 1.
Sl st in base of leaf, ch5, sl st in each of next 5 ch, sl st in base of leaf.
Fasten off.

IVY STEM

Using 2 strands of D held tog and US size C/2–D/3 (3mm) hook, ch250. Fasten off.

MAKING UP AND FINISHING

To finish each bird, sew a wing on each side with the pointed end toward the front. Use black embroidery thread to sew French knots (see page 123) for the eyes. Use the long tail on the beak to secure the beak shape, then sew a beak onto each bird.

To finish the nest, roll the top edge down into the inside to create a double edge all around the nest. Hold in place with a few stitches.

Block each ivy leaf.

Start by wrapping the long stem all around the wreath. Join the two ends together and secure in place. Position your ivy leaves and then stick them in place with a glue gun. Add the eggs to the nest, sticking them in place with a dot of glue. Sit one bird on top of the eggs and glue in place. Hang the second bird from the top of the wreath using invisible nylon thread.

Add a hanging loop and a decorative bow in a coordinating color of ribbon.

Together sunflowers and poppies create instant sunshine, with the two bright colors sitting together beautifully. On this wreath the addition of a length of wired artificial ivy gives the perfect dark contrast for these two flowers to look their very best.

sunflower and poppy wreath

FOR THE WREATH

SUNFLOWER CENTER TOP (make 5)

Round 1: Using A, make a magic ring, 6sc into the ring.
Work in a continuous spiral. PM in last st and move up as each round is finished.
Round 2: 2sc in each st to end. *12 sts.*
Round 3: *1sc, 2sc in next st; rep from * to end. *18 sts.*
Round 4: *1sc in each of next 2 sts, 2sc in next st; rep from * to end. *24 sts.*
Round 5: *1sc in each of next 3 sts, 2sc in next st; rep from * to end. *30 sts.*
Round 6: 1sc in each st to end, join with a sl st in first st.
Fasten off.

SKILL RATING: ● ● ●

MATERIALS:

Paintbox Yarns Wool Mix Aran (50% acrylic, 50% wool. approx. 180m/ 196yds per 3½oz/100g ball) worsted (Aran) weight yarn
  1 ball each of shades:
    Soft Fudge 809 (A)
    Mustard Yellow 823 (B)
    Pillar Red 814 (C)

US size E/4 (3.5mm) crochet hook

Stitch marker

Yarn needle

Polyester toy stuffing

Black fiber tip pen

16in (40cm) diameter twig wreath

Approx. 56in (140cm) length of wired artificial ivy

Pins

Hot glue gun

Ribbon for hanging loop

FINISHED MEASUREMENTS:

Each poppy: 2¼in (6cm)

Wreath: 16in (40cm) diameter

GAUGE (TENSION):

15 sts x 15 rows = 3 x 2¾in (7.5 x 7cm) working single crochet, using a US size E/4 (3.5mm) crochet hook.

ABBREVIATIONS:

See page 127.

The poppy is worked in sets of two petals, two being worked into the front loop only of the 6 sts from the magic ring, and two being worked into the back loop only of the 6 sts from the magic ring. The back petals are positioned to alternate with the front petals.

SUNFLOWER CENTER BASE (make 5)

Round 1: Using A make a magic ring, 6sc into the ring. Work in a continuous spiral. PM in last st and move up as each round is finished.
Round 2: 2sc in each st to end. *12 sts.*
Round 3: *1sc, 2sc in next st; rep from * to end. *18 sts.*
Round 4: *1sc in each of next 2 sts, 2sc in next st; rep from * to end. *24 sts.*
Round 5: *1sc in each of next 3 sts, 2sc in next st; rep from * to end, join with a sl st in first st. *30 sts.*
Fasten off.

SUNFLOWER PETALS (make 5)

Using B, ch81.
Row 1: Sl st in 2nd ch from hook, *sl st in next st, ch8, 1sc in 2nd ch from hook, 1sc in each of next 2 ch, 1hdc in each of next 4 ch, skip 1 ch, sl st in next ch; rep from * to end, sl st in last ch.
Fasten off.

POPPY (make 10)

Round 1: Using C, make a magic ring, 6sc into the ring, join with a sl st in first st.
Make first front petal:
Row 1: Ch1, 2sc in FLO of each of first 3 sts, turn. *6 sts.*
Row 2: Ch1, *2sc in next st, 1sc; rep from * to end, turn. *9 sts.*
Row 3: Ch1, *sc2tog, 1sc; rep from * to end, turn. *6 sts.*
Row 4: Ch1, *sc2tog, 1sc; rep from * to end, turn. *4 sts.*
Row 5: Ch1, [sc2tog] to end. *2 sts.*
Fasten off.
Make second front petal:
Working in FLO only of 3 rem sts in magic ring, repeat as for first petal.
Make back petals:
Work as for front petals but work into BLO of 6 sts in magic ring. When starting first back petal, position it to alt with top petals.
Fasten off.

MAKING UP AND FINISHING

Once the sunflower petals have been blocked, carefully wrap a strip of petals all the way around each center top and stitch in place. Stitch the center base onto the bottom of the flower, adding a small amount of stuffing before fastening off.

To complete the poppies, use a black fiber tip pen to color in the center of each flower.

Begin by twisting the length of ivy around the wreath. Lay the wreath on a flat surface and use blocking pins to position the sunflowers and poppies where you want them to be. Glue firmly in place with a hot glue gun.

To finish off the wreath, add a hanging loop at the top of the wreath and stitch or glue in place.

This bobbly heart wreath could not be simpler to make. It adds a beautiful touch to any room in the house, with the bead colors being easy to change to coordinate with any décor. The beads are threaded onto a length of elastic thread, making it easier to attach them to the wreath base.

bobbly heart wreath

SKILL RATING: ● ● ●

MATERIALS:

Sublime Baby Cashmerino Silk DK (75% merino wool, 20% silk, 5% cashmere, approx. 127yds/116m per 1¾oz/50g ball) light worsted (DK) weight yarn
  1 ball each of shades:
    Vanilla 003 (A)
    Pebble 006 (B)
    Flopsy 573 (C)
    Little Duck Egg 436 (D)

US size C/2–D/3 (3mm) crochet hook

Stitch marker

Yarn needle

Polyester toy stuffing

Elastic thread

10½ x 10in (26 x 25cm) wicker heart

Pins

Hot glue gun

Ribbon for hanging loop

FINISHED MEASUREMENTS:

Each bead: approx. 1in (2.5cm) diameter

Wreath: 10½ x 10in (26 x 25cm)

GAUGE (TENSION):

15 sts x 15 rows = 2½ x 2⅜in (6.5 x 6cm) working single crochet, using a US size C/2–D/3 (3mm) crochet hook.

ABBREVIATIONS:

See page 127.

FOR THE WREATH

BOBBLE (make 9 in A, C and D, 10 in B)

Round 1: Using A, B, C or D, make a magic ring, 4sc into the ring. Work in a continuous spiral. PM in last st and move up as each round is finished.

Round 2: 2sc in each st to end. *8 sts.*

Round 3: *1sc, 2sc in next st; rep from * to end. *12 sts.*

Round 4: *1sc in each of next 2 sts, 2sc in next st; rep from * to end. *16 sts.*

Round 5: 1sc in each st to end.

Round 6: *1sc in each of next 2 sts, sc2tog; rep from * to end. *12 sts.*

Round 7: *1sc in next st, sc2tog; rep from * to end. *8 sts.*
Stuff the bead.

Round 8: [Sc2tog] to end. *4 sts.*
Fasten off, using long end to gather and close hole.

MAKING UP AND FINISHING

Keeping the color sequence correct, thread each bead onto the elastic thread. Once all the beads are joined together, position them on the wreath base, holding with blocking pins. Stick the string of beads to the wreath with a hot glue gun.

Attach a hanging loop made with coordinating ribbon.

CHAPTER 4

CHRISTMAS

This stylish and simple wreath will add a festive feel to any room over the Christmas season—and with the leaves being quick and simple to make, you'll find yourself making them for friends and loved ones, too!

mistletoe wreath

SKILL RATING: ● ● ●

MATERIALS:

Cascade Sunseeker (47% cotton, 48% acrylic, 5% metallic, approx. 237yds/217m per 3½oz/100g ball) light worsted (DK) weight yarn
  1 ball each of shades:
    Watercress 43 (A)
    White 35 (B)

US size C/2–D/3 (3mm) crochet hook

Yarn needle

10in (25cm) diameter wicker wreath, sprayed with artificial snow

Hot glue gun

Ribbon for a hanging loop

FINISHED MEASUREMENTS:

Wreath: 10in (25cm) diameter

Each mistletoe (beg of stem to tip of leaf): 2¾in (7cm)

GAUGE (TENSION):

15 sts x 15 rows = 2¾ x 2½in (7 x 6.5cm) working single crochet, using a US size C/2–D/3 (3mm) crochet hook.

ABBREVIATIONS:

See page 127.

FOR THE WREATH

MISTLETOE (make 10)

Using A, ch11.

Leaf 1: Sl st in 2nd ch from hook, sl st in each of next 3 ch, 1sc in each of next 4 ch, 1hdc, 2hdc in the last ch, do not turn, working back down other side of ch, 1hdc in each of first 4 ch, 1sc in each of next 3 ch, sl st in each of last 3 ch.

Stalk: Ch12, sl st in 2nd ch from hook, sl st in each of next 10 ch, ending at base of leaf 1.

Leaf 2: Ch11, 1hdc in 2nd ch from hook, 1hdc in each of next 4 ch, 1sc in each of next 3 ch, sl st in each of last 2 ch, do not turn, ch1, working back down other side of ch, skip first ch, sl st in each of next 2 ch, 1sc in each of next 4 ch, 1hdc in each of last 3 ch, join with a sl st in first st. Fasten off.

MAKING UP AND FINISHING

To complete each mistletoe sprig, embroider 2 to 3 French knots (see page 123) in B where the two leaves meet at the bottom. The knots will also serve to hold the leaves together.

Use a hot glue gun to stick the leaves into position. Finish the wreath by adding a hanging loop in coordinating ribbon.

MATERIALS:

Cascade Sunseeker (47% cotton, 48% acrylic, 5% metallic, approx. 237yds/217m per 3½oz/100g ball) light worsted (DK) weight yarn
  1 ball each of shades:
    Watercress 43 (A)
    Cherry 42 (B)

Classic Elite Yarns Ava (86% wool, 9% viscose, 5% metallized polyester, 128yds/117m per 1¾oz/50g ball) light worsted (DK) weight yarn
  1 ball of shade Gold 6850 (C)

Gold embroidery thread

US size C/2–D/3 (3mm) and US size B/1 (2mm) crochet hooks

Stitch marker

Yarn needle

Polyester toy stuffing

Black embroidery thread

11½in (30cm) diameter wicker wreath

Pins

Hot glue gun

Ribbon for hanging loop and bow

FINISHED MEASUREMENTS:

Wreath: 11½in (30cm) diameter

Each holly leaf: 2¾in (7cm)

GAUGE (TENSION):

15 sts x 15 rows = 2¾ x 2½in (7 x 6.5cm) working single crochet, using a US size C/2–D/3 (3mm) hook and Cascade Sunseeker.

15 sts x 15 rows = 2⅜in (6cm) square working single crochet, using a US size C/2–D/3 (3mm) crochet hook and Classic Elite Yarns Ava.

ABBREVIATIONS:

See page 127.

Dark green holly leaves, with their burst of bright red berries, give these golden Christmas birds a perfect bower to nestle in. The birds are worked in yarn that has a metallic thread in it, so they catch the light beautifully against the contrast of the natural twig wreath.

holly wreath with gold birds

FOR THE WREATH

HOLLY LEAF (make 17)

Using A and US size C/2–D/3 (3mm) hook, ch12.

Round 1: 1sc in 2nd ch from hook, 1sc in next ch, 1hdc in each of next 3 ch, 1dc in each of next 2 ch, 1hdc in each of next 2 ch, 1sc in each of last 2 ch, do not turn, ch1, working back down other side of ch, skip first ch, 1sc in each of first 2 ch, 1hdc in each of next 3 ch, 1dc in each of next 2 ch, 1hdc in each of next 2 ch, 1sc in last ch, ch6, sl st in each ch to base of leaf, sl st in bottom of leaf to join.

Round 2:

Point 1: Sl st in next st of leaf, ch2, sl st in 2nd ch from hook, sl st in next st on leaf.

Point 2: 1sc in next st of leaf, ch2, sl st in 2nd ch from hook, sl st in next st on leaf.

Point 3: 1sc in next st of leaf, ch3, sl st in 3rd ch from hook, sl st in next st on leaf.

Point 4: 1sc in next st of leaf, ch2, sl st in 2nd ch from hook, sl st in next st on leaf.

Point 5: Sl st in next st of leaf, ch2, sl st in 2nd ch from hook, sl st in next st on leaf.

Point 6: Sl st in top st of leaf, ch3, sl st in 2nd ch from hook, sl st in top st of leaf.

Point 7: Rep point 5.
Point 8: Rep point 4.
Point 9: Rep point 3.
Point 10: Rep point 2.
Point 11: Rep point 1, join with a sl st in base of leaf.
Fasten off.

HOLLY BERRY (make 16)

Round 1: Using B and US size C/2–D/3 (3mm) hook, make a magic ring, 3sc into the ring.
Work in a continuous spiral, do not join.
Round 2: 2sc in each st to end. *6 sts.*
Round 3: [Sc2tog] to end.
Fasten off, using long end to gather and close hole.

Round 17: 1sc in each of first 3 sts, [sc2tog] twice and stop. Join 2 sides tog along bottom of bird with a sc seam, working 6sc.
Lightly stuff head and bottom curve of body.

Make the tail:
Row 1: Flatten end of bird, ch1, 4sc evenly across tail end, turn.
Row 2: Ch1, 2sc in each st to end, turn. *8 sts.*
Row 3: Ch1, sl st in first st, skip next 2 sts, (1sc, 1hdc, 1dc, 1tr) in next st, ch2, sl st in 2nd ch from hook, (1tr, 1dc, 1hdc, 1sc) in next st, skip 2 sts, sl st in last st.
Fasten off.

WING 1 (make 2)
Using C and US size C/2–D/3 (3mm) hook, ch7.
Row 1: 1sc in 2nd ch from hook, 1sc in next ch, 1hdc in each of next 2 ch, 1dc in each of next 2 ch (3dc, 1sc) in last ch, do not turn, working back down other side of ch, 1sc in each of next 5 ch, join with a sl st in first st.
Fasten off.

WING 2 (make 2)
Using C and US size C/2–D/3 (3mm) hook, ch7.
Row 1: 1sc in 2nd ch from hook, 1sc in each of next 5ch, do not turn, working back down other side of ch, 4dc in same ch as last sc, 1dc in next ch, 1hdc in each of next 2 ch, 1sc in each of next 2 ch, join with a sl st in first st.
Fasten off.

BEAK (make 2)
Using gold embroidery thread and US size B/1 (2mm) hook, ch2.
Row 1: 2sc in 2nd ch from hook, turn. *2 sts.*
Row 2: Ch1, 1sc in first st, 2sc in last st, turn. *3 sts.*
Row 3: Ch1, 2sc in first st, 1sc, 2sc in last st, turn. *5 sts.*
Row 4: Ch1, 2sc in first st, 1sc in each of next 3 sts, 2sc in last st. *7 sts.*
Fasten off, leaving a long tail.

MAKING UP AND FINISHING

Block the leaves.

To finish each bird, sew a wing on each side with the pointed end toward the front. Sew the eyes using black embroidery thread. Use the long end to secure the beak shape, then sew each beak to a bird.

Lay the wreath on a flat surface and use blocking pins to position the leaves, berries and birds where you want them to be. Glue firmly in place with a hot glue gun.

To finish off the wreath, add a hanging loop and bow at the top of the wreath and stitch or glue in place.

BIRD (make 2)

Round 1: Using C and US size C/2–D/3 (3mm) hook, make a magic ring, 6sc into the ring.
Work in a continuous spiral. PM in last st and move up as each round is finished.
Round 2: 2sc in each st to end. *12 sts.*
Round 3: *1sc, 2sc in next st; rep from * to end. *18 sts.*
Rounds 4 to 6: 1sc in each st to end.
Round 7: 1sc in each of first 10 sts, 2sc in next st, 1sc in each of next 2 sts, 2sc in next st, 1sc in each of last 4 sts. *20 sts.*
Round 8: 1sc in each of first 12 sts, [2sc in next st, 1sc in next st] 4 times. *24 sts.*
Round 9: 1sc in each st to end.
Round 10: 1sc in each of first 15 sts, [2sc in next st, 1sc in each of next 2 sts] 3 times. *27 sts.*
Round 11: 1sc in each of first 14 sts, 2sc in next st, 1sc in each of next 3 sts, 1hdc in each of next 5 sts, 1sc in each of next 3 sts, 2sc in last st. *29 sts.*
Round 12: 1sc in each of first 4 sts, sc2tog, 1sc, sc2tog, 1sc in each of next 9 sts, 2sc in next st, 1sc in each of next 2 sts, 2sc in next st, 1sc in each of last 7 sts. *29 sts.*
Round 13: 1sc in each of first 5 sts, sc2tog, 1sc in each of next 5 sts, 2sc in next st, 1sc in each of next 2 sts, 2sc in next st, 1sc in each of next 3 sts, 1hdc, 1sc in each of next 2 sts, 2sc in next st, 1sc in each of last 6 sts. *31 sts.*
Round 14: 1sc in each of first 5 sts, [sc2tog] twice, 1sc in each of next 10 sts, 1hdc in each of next 6 sts, 1sc in each of last 6 sts. *29 sts.*
Round 15: 1sc in each of first 4 sts, [sc2tog] twice, 1sc, sc2tog, 1sc in each of last 18 sts. *26 sts.*
Round 16: 1sc in each of first 2 sts, [sc2tog] 4 times, 1sc in each of next 5 sts, 1hdc in each of next 8 sts, 1sc in each of last 3 sts. *22 sts.*

Brightly colored baubles are the perfect decoration to mark the beginning of the festive season—and this wreath allows you to display them anywhere in your home. All the baubles have a touch of glitter and some have added metallic spots.

christmas bauble wreath

SKILL RATING: ● ● ○

MATERIALS:

Cascade Sunseeker (48% acrylic, 47% cotton, 5% metallic, approx. 237yds/217m per 3½oz/100g ball) light worsted (DK) weight yarn
    1 ball each of shades:
        Cherry 42 (A)
        Daiquiri Green 33 (B)
        Silver 04 (C)

Anchor Artiste Metallic (80% viscose, 20% polyester, approx. 109yds/100m per ⅞oz/25g ball) thread
    1 ball of White 304 (D)

US size C/2–D/3 (3mm) crochet hook

Stitch marker

6 polystyrene balls, 2in (50mm) diameter

10 polystyrene balls, 1½in (40mm) diameter

12in (30cm) diameter twig wreath

Hot glue gun

Coordinating ribbon for hanging loop

FINISHED MEASUREMENTS:

Wreath: 12in (30cm) diameter

GAUGE (TENSION):

15 sts x 15 rows = 2¾ x 2½in (7 x 6.5cm) working single crochet, using a US size C/2–D/3 (3mm) crochet hook and Cascade Sunseeker.

ABBREVIATIONS:

See page 127.

FOR THE WREATH

LARGE BAUBLE (make 2 in each of A, B and C)

Round 1: Using either A, B or C, make a magic ring, 6sc into the ring.

Work in a continuous spiral. PM in last st and move up as each round is finished.

Round 2: 2sc in each st to end. *12 sts.*

Round 3: *1sc, 2sc in next st; rep from * to end. *18 sts.*

Round 4: *1sc in each of next 2 sts, 2sc in next st; rep from * to end. *24 sts.*

Round 5: *1sc in each of next 3 sts, 2sc in next st; rep from * to end. *30 sts.*

Round 6: *1sc in each of next 4 sts, 2sc in next st; rep from * to end. *36 sts.*

Rounds 7 to 13: 1sc in each st to end.

Insert 2in (50mm) polystyrene ball.

Round 14: *1sc in each of next 4 sts, sc2tog; rep from * to end. *30 sts.*

Round 15: *1sc in each of next 3 sts, sc2tog; rep from * to end. *24 sts.*

Round 16: *1sc in each of next 2 sts, sc2tog; rep from * to end. *18 sts.*

Rounds 17 and 18: 1sc in each st to end.

Round 19: *1sc, sc2tog; rep from * to end. *12 sts.*

Round 20: 1sc in each st to end.

Round 21: [Sc2tog] to end.

Fasten off.

MEDIUM BAUBLE (make 4 in A, 3 in B, 3 in C)

Round 1: Using either A, B or C, make a magic ring, 5sc into the ring.

Round 2: 2sc in each st to end. *10 sts.*

Round 3: *1sc, 2sc in next st; rep from * to end. *15 sts.*

Round 4: *1sc in each of next 2 sts, 2sc in next st; rep from * to end. *20 sts.*

Round 5: *1sc in each of next 3 sts, 2sc in next st; rep from * to end. *25 sts.*

Round 6: *1sc in each of next 4 sts, 2sc in next st; rep from * to end. *30 sts.*

Rounds 7 to 11: 1sc in each st to end.

Insert 1½in (40mm) polystyrene ball.

Round 12: *1sc in each of next 4 sts, sc2tog; rep from * to end. *25 sts.*

Round 13: *1sc in each of next 3 sts, sc2tog; rep from * to end. *20 sts.*

Rounds 14 and 15: 1sc in each st to end.

Round 16: *1sc in each of next 2 sts, sc2tog; rep from * to end. *15 sts.*

Round 17: *1sc, sc2tog; rep from * to end. *10 sts.*

Round 18: [Sc2tog] to end.

Fasten off.

MAKING UP AND FINISHING

Using D, add French knots (see page 123) to one of each of the 2in (50mm) baubles in A, B and C, and to two of each of the 1½in (40mm) baubles in A, B and C.

Lay the wreath on a flat surface and use blocking pins to position the baubles where you want them to be. Glue firmly in place with a hot glue gun.

To finish off the wreath, add a coordinating ribbon and hanging loop at the top and stitch or glue in place.

Christmas trees come in all shapes and sizes—and these miniature ones are the perfect size to be strung on some bright cord and hung along a shelf or fireplace throughout the festive season. As a bright color contrast, glittering red stars hang between each tree.

christmas garland

SKILL RATING: ● ● ●

MATERIALS:

Cascade Sunseeker (48% acrylic, 47% cotton, 5% metallic, approx. 237yds/217m per 3½oz/100g ball) light worsted (DK) weight yarn
    1 ball each of shades:
        Cherry 42 (A)
        Watercress 43 (B)
        Clover 31 (C)
        Limestone 27 (D)

Anchor Artiste Metallic (80% viscose, 20% polyester, approx. 109yds/100m per ⅞oz /25g ball) thread
    1 ball each of shades:
        Gold 300 (E)
        Red 318 (F)

US size C/2–D/3 (3mm) and US size B/1 (2mm) crochet hooks

Stitch marker

Polyester toy stuffing

Needle and matching thread

Thin string for hanging loops

70in (175cm) red cord

Coordinating ribbon for bows

FINISHED MEASUREMENTS:

Each tree: 5¼in (13cm) high

Each large star: 2½in (6.5cm) from point to opposite point

Each small star: 1¾in (2cm) from point to opposite point

Garland: approx. 54in (135cm) long

GAUGE (TENSION):

15 sts x 15 rows = 2¾ x 2½in (7 x 6.5cm) working single crochet, using a US size C/2–D/3 (3mm) crochet hook and Cascade Sunseeker.

ABBREVIATIONS:

See page 127.

FOR THE GARLAND

TREE (make 3 in B, 4 in C with base in D)

Make the base:
Round 1: Using D and US size C/2–D/3 (3mm) hook, make a magic ring, 6sc into the ring.
Round 2: 2sc in each st to end, join with a sl st in first st. *12 sts.*
Round 3: Ch1, 12sc BLO, join with a sl st in first st.
Rounds 4 to 8: Ch1, working in both loops as normal, 1sc in each st to end, join with a sl st in first st.
Round 9: Ch1 (does not count as st throughout), 2hdc in each st to end, join with a sl st in first st. *24 sts.*
Round 10: Ch1, *1hdc in next st, 2hdc in next st; rep from * to end, join with a sl st in first st. *36 sts.*
Round 11: Join in either B or C, ch1, 1sc in each st to end, join with a sl st in first st
Round 12: Ch1, 1sc BLO in each st to end.
Work in a continuous spiral. PM in last st and move up as each round is finished.
Make the tree:
Rounds 13 to 15: 1sc in each st to end. *36 sts.*
Round 16: *1sc in each of next 7 sts, sc2tog; rep from * to end. *32 sts.*
Rounds 17 to 19: 1sc in each st to end.
Round 20: *1sc in each of next 6 sts, sc2tog; rep from * to end. *28 sts.*
Rounds 21 and 22: 1sc in each st to end.
Round 23: *1sc in each of next 5 sts, sc2tog; rep from * to end. *24 sts.*
Round 24: 1sc in each st to end.
Round 25: *1sc in each of next 4 sts, sc2tog; rep from * to end. *20 sts.*
Round 26: 1sc in each st to end.
Round 27: *1sc in each of next 3 sts, sc2tog; rep from * to end. *16 sts.*
Round 28: 1sc in each st to end.
Round 29: *1sc in each of next 2 sts, sc2tog; rep from * to end. *12 sts.*
Round 30: 1sc in each st to end.
Stuff the tree.
Round 31: *1sc, sc2tog; rep from * to end. *8 sts.*
Round 32: 1sc in each st to end.
Round 33: [Sc2tog] to end. *4 sts.*
Round 34: 1sc in each st to end.
Round 35: [Sc2tog] twice. *2 sts.*
Fasten off.

RUFFLE EDGING (make one for each tree in matching yarn)
Using US size C/2–D/3 (3mm) hook, ch151.
Starting in 2nd ch from hook, *(1sc, 1hdc) in next ch, (1hdc, 1sc) in next ch, sl st in next ch; rep from * to end. Fasten off.

LARGE STAR (make 16)
Round 1: Using A and US size C/2–D/3 (3mm) hook, make a magic ring, 5sc into the ring.
Work in a continuous spiral, do not join.
Round 2: 2sc in each st to end. *10 sts.*
Round 3: *1sc, 2sc in next st; rep from * to end, join with a sl st in first st. *15 sts.*
Round 4: *Ch7, sl st in 2nd ch from hook, 1sc in next ch, 1hdc in next ch, 1dc in next ch, 1tr in next ch, skip last ch and next 2 sts of center, sl st in next st of center; rep from * 4 more times around (5 points), ending last point with sl st in base of first point.
Fasten off.

SMALL STAR (make 7)
Round 1: Using E and US size B/1 (2mm) hook, make a magic ring, 5sc into the ring, join with a sl st in first st.
Round 2: *Ch3, sl st in 2nd ch from hook, 1sc in next ch, sl st in next st of center; rep from * 4 more times around (5 points), ending last point with sl st in base of first point.
Fasten off.

MAKING UP AND FINISHING

Place two of the large stars WS together and use a needle and yarn to oversew together all around the edge.

Using E or F, add French knots (see page 123) along the ruffle edging for each tree. Wind the ruffle all the way around the tree and pin to hold. Stitch in place securely with a needle and thread.
Stitch one small gold star to the top of each tree.

Make a hanging loop in thin string and stitch onto each tree and large star. Thread the trees and large stars onto the cord and stitch in place with a needle and thread to stop them slipping along the cord.

Add coordinating bows at each end of the garland and stitch in place.

MATERIALS:

Schachenmayr Catania (100% cotton, approx. 137yds/125m per 1¾oz/50g ball) sport (5 ply) weight yarn
   1 ball each of shades:
      Kamel 0179 (A)
      Signalrot 0115 (B)

US size B/1–C/2 (2.5mm) crochet hook

Stitch marker

10 toy safety eyes, ⅛in (3mm) size

Polyester toy stuffing

4 pipe cleaners, 12in (30cm) long

Needle and matching thread

4 green buttons, ⅛in (3mm) diameter

6 red buttons, ⅛in (3mm) diameter

5 small red ribbon bows

Red embroidery thread

Pins

Thin string for hanging loops

60in (150cm) gold cord

4 short lengths of narrow green velvet ribbon

2 lengths of wide green velvet ribbon

FINISHED MEASUREMENTS:

Each gingerbread man: 3¼in (8cm) tall

Each candy cane: 2¾in (7cm) long, with top turned over

Garland: approx. 41½in (105cm) long

GAUGE (TENSION):

15 sts x 15 rows = 2½in (6.5cm) square working single crochet, using a US size B/1–C/2 (2.5mm) crochet hook.

ABBREVIATIONS:

See page 127.

You may not get the delicious smell of warm gingerbread cooking while making this garland, but these little gingerbread men and candy canes will last and last and can be brought out every year to decorate your home at Christmas time.

gingerbread garland

FOR THE GARLAND

GINGERBREAD MEN (make 5)

Round 1: Using A, make a magic ring, 6sc into the ring.
Work in a continuous spiral. PM in last st and move up as each round is finished.
Round 2: 2sc in each st to end. *12 sts.*
Round 3: *1sc, 2sc in next st; rep from * to end. *18 sts.*
Round 4: *1sc in each of next 2 sts, 2sc in next st; rep from * to end. *24 sts.*

Rounds 5 to 7: 1sc in each st to end.
Attach safety eyes, approx. 3 sts apart.
Round 8: *1sc in each of next 2 sts, sc2tog; rep from * to end. *18 sts.*
Round 9: *1sc in next st, sc2tog; rep from * to end. *12 sts.*
Round 10: *1sc in next st, sc2tog; rep from * to end. *8 sts.*
Round 11: 2sc in each of next 7 sts, 1sc in last st. *15 sts.*
Round 12: *1sc in each of next 2 sts, 2sc in next st; rep from * to end. *20 sts.*
Rounds 13 to 22: 1sc in each st to end.
Fasten off.
Make the legs:
Lay gingerbread man flat, re-join A to center of front body and join two bottom edges in center by working 1sc from front to back working through both edges, dividing the bottom opening into two equal leg openings.
Stuff body very lightly.
First leg round 23: 9sc around one leg opening.
Work in a continuous spiral. PM in last st and move up as each round is finished.
First leg rounds 24 to 27: 1sc in each st to end. *9 sts.*
Stuff leg very lightly.
Round 28: [Sc2tog] to end.
Fasten off.
Second leg: Work as first leg.

ARMS (make 2 for each man)
Round 1: Using A, make a magic ring, 4sc into the ring.
Work in a continuous spiral. PM in last st and move up as each round is finished.
Round 2: 2sc in each st to end. *8 sts.*
Rounds 3 to 10: 1sc in each st to end.
Fasten off.

CANDY CANE (make 4)
Round 1: Using A, make a magic ring, 4sc into the ring. Work in a continuous spiral. PM in last st and move up as each round is finished.
Round 2: 2sc in each st to end. *8 sts.*
Rounds 3 to 25: 1sc in each st to end.
Fold a pipe cleaner into three and carefully push inside cane.
Round 26: [Sc2tog] to end.
Fasten off.

CANDY CANE STRIPE (make 4)
Using B, ch80.
Fasten off.

MAKING UP AND FINISHING

Sew the arms and buttons onto each gingerbread men. Stitch on small red bows for bow ties. Using red embroidery thread, stitch on the mouth.

Turn over the top part of the candy cane to make the hook shape and then wind the stripe all the way around it, pinning in place to hold. Use a needle and thread to stitch into place securely.

Cut short lengths of thin string, thread one through the top of each gingerbread man and cane and knot to make a hanging loop. Thread the gingerbread men and candy canes onto the cord and stitch in place with a needle and thread to stop them slipping along the cord. Tie the narrow green velvet ribbons into bows and sew one above each candy cane.

Add coordinating bows in wider ribbon at each end of the garland and stitch in place.

SKILL RATING: ● ● ●

MATERIALS:

Cascade Sunseeker (48% acrylic, 47% cotton, 5% metallic, approx. 237yds/217m per 3½oz/100g ball) DK (light worsted) weight yarn
  1 ball of White 35 (A)

Schachenmayr Catania (100% cotton, approx. 137yds/125m per 1¾oz/50g ball) sport (5 ply) weight yarn
  1 ball each of shades:
    Kamel 0179 (B)
    Zimt 0383 (C)

Anchor Artiste Metallic (80% viscose, 20% polyester, approx. 109yds/100m per ⅞oz/25g ball) thread
  1 ball each of shades:
    Emerald Green 322 (D)
    Red 318 (E)

US size B/1–C/2 (2.5mm) and US size B/1 (2mm) crochet hooks

Stitch marker

Yarn needle

FINISHED MEASUREMENTS:

Each snowball/pudding: 5in (12.5cm) circumference

Each holly leaf: 1¼in (1.5cm) long

GAUGE (TENSION):

15 sts x 15 rows = 2¾ x 2⅜in (7 x 6cm) working single crochet, using a US size B/1–C/2 (2.5mm) crochet hook and Cascade Sunseeker.

15 sts x 15 rows = 2⅜in (6cm) square working single crochet, using a US size B/1–C/2 (2.5mm) crochet hook and Schachenmayr Catania.

ABBREVIATIONS:

See page 127.

Make the gift of a simple wrapped chocolate into something special with these cute covers, designed as a snowball or as a Christmas pudding. They'd look great as decoration or favors on a festive table, too.

christmas puddings and snowballs

FOR THE COVERS

SNOWBALL BASE

Round 1: Using US size B/1–C/2 (2.5mm) hook and A, make a magic ring, 6sc into the ring.
Work in a continuous spiral. PM in last st and move up as each round is finished.
Round 2: 2sc in each st to end. *12 sts.*
Round 3: *1sc, 2sc in next st; rep from * to end. *18 sts.*
Round 4: *1sc in each of next 2 sts, 2sc in next st; rep from * to end. *24 sts.*
Round 5: 1sc in each st to end.
Round 6: *1sc in each of next 3 sts, 2sc in next st; rep from * to end. *30 sts.*
Rounds 7 and 8: 1sc in each st to end.
Join last round with a sl st in first st.
Fasten off.

SNOWBALL TOP

Round 1: Using US size B/1–C/2 (2.5mm) hook and A, make a magic ring, 6sc into the ring.
Work in a continuous spiral. PM in last st and move up as each round is finished.

Round 2: 2sc in each st to end. *12 sts.*

Round 3: *1sc, 2sc in next st; rep from * to end. *18 sts.*

Round 4: *1sc in each of next 2 sts, 2sc in next st; rep from * to end. *24 sts.*

Round 5: 1sc in each st to end.

Round 6: *1sc in each of next 3 sts, 2sc in next st; rep from * to end. *30 sts.*

Rounds 7 and 8: 1sc in each st to end.

Round 9: 1sc in each st to end, join with a sl st in first st.
Fasten off.

CHRISTMAS PUDDING BASE

Using US size B/1–C/2 (2.5mm) hook and B, work as for snowball base.

CHRISTMAS PUDDING TOP

Using US size B/1–C/2 (2.5mm) hook and A, work as for snowball top rounds 1 to 8.

Round 9: *(1hdc, 1dc) in next st, (1dc, 1hdc) in next st, sl st in each of next 2 sts; rep from * to end, ending final rep with (1dc, 1hdc, sl st) in last st, join with a sl st in first st.
Fasten off.

HOLLY LEAF (make 2 per pudding/snowball)

Using US size B/1 (2mm) crochet hook and D, ch6.

Round 1: Sl st in 2nd ch from hook, [1hdc in next ch, sl st in next ch] twice, ch1 across bottom of leaf, do not turn, working back down other side of ch, sl st in each of next 2 ch, 1hdc in next ch, sl st in next ch, join with a sl st in first st.
Fasten off.

MAKING UP AND FINISHING

For each Christmas pudding/snowball, place a top and base around each chocolate. At the back of the cover, oversew a few stitches in yarn to create a hinge.

Sew two holly leaves to the top of each Christmas pudding/snowball. Using E, add French knots (see page 123) to create three holly berries between the leaves. Using C, add French knots to the base of each Christmas pudding.

techniques

In this section, we explain how to master the simple crochet and finishing techniques that you need to make the projects in this book.

Holding the hook

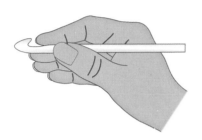

Pick up your hook as though you are picking up a pen or pencil. Keeping the hook held loosely between your fingers and thumb, turn your hand so that the palm is facing up and the hook is balanced in your hand and resting in the space between your index finger and your thumb.

You can also hold the hook like a knife—this may be easier if you are working with a large hook or with chunky yarn. Choose the method that you find most comfortable.

Holding the yarn

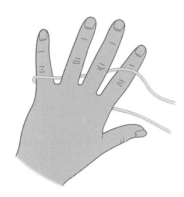

1 Pick up the yarn with your little finger in the opposite hand to your hook, with your palm facing upward and with the short end in front. Turn your hand to face downward, with the yarn on top of your index finger and under the other two fingers and wrapped right around the little finger, as shown above.

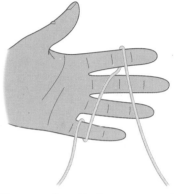

2 Turn your hand to face you, ready to hold the work in your middle finger and thumb. Keeping your index finger only at a slight curve, hold the work or the slip knot using the same hand, between your middle finger and your thumb and just below the crochet hook and loop/s on the hook.

Making a slip knot

The simplest way is to make a circle with the yarn, so that the loop is facing downward.

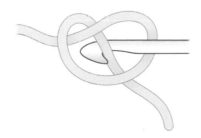

1 In one hand hold the circle at the top where the yarn crosses, and let the tail drop down at the back so that it falls across the center of the loop. With your free hand or the tip of a crochet hook, pull a loop through the circle.

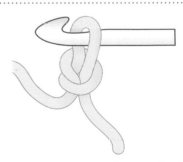

2 Put the hook into the loop and pull gently so that it forms a loose loop on the hook.

Yarn over hook (yoh)

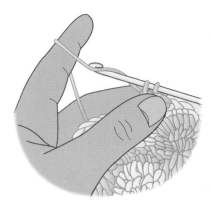

To create a stitch, catch the yarn from behind with the hook pointing upward. As you gently pull the yarn through the loop on the hook, turn the hook so it faces downward and slide the yarn through the loop. The loop on the hook should be kept loose enough for the hook to slide through easily.

Magic ring

This is a useful starting technique if you do not want a visible hole in the center of your round. Loop the yarn around your finger, insert the hook through the ring, yarn round hook, pull through the ring to make the first chain. Work the number of stitches required into the ring and then pull the end to tighten the center ring and close the hole.

Chain (ch)

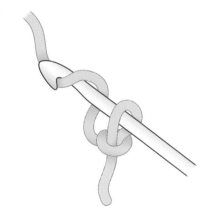

1 Using the hook, wrap the yarn over the hook ready to pull it through the loop on the hook.

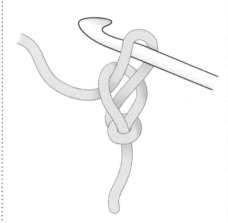

2 Pull through, creating a new loop on the hook. Continue in this way to create a chain of the required length.

Chain ring

If you are crocheting a round shape, one way of starting off is by crocheting a number of chains following the instructions in your pattern, and then joining them into a circle.

1 To join the chain into a circle, insert the crochet hook into the first chain that you made (not into the slip knot), yarn over hook.

2 Pull the yarn through the chain and through the loop on your hook at the same time, thereby creating a slip stitch and forming a circle. You now have a chain ring ready to work stitches into as instructed in the pattern.

Chain space (ch sp)

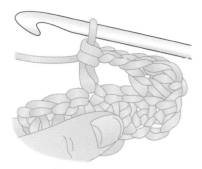

1 A chain space is the space that has been made under a chain in the previous round or row, and falls in between other stitches.

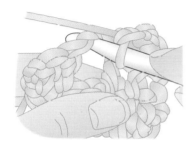

2 Stitches into a chain space are made directly into the hole created under the chain and not into the chain stitches themselves.

Slip stitch (sl st)

A slip stitch doesn't create any height and is often used as the last stitch to create a smooth and even round or row.

1 To make a slip stitch: first put the hook through the work, yarn over hook.

2 Pull the yarn through both the work and through the loop on the hook at the same time, so you will have 1 loop on the hook.

Making rounds

When working in rounds the work is not turned, so you are always working from one side. Depending on the pattern you are working, a "round" can be square. Start each round by making one or more chains to create the height you need for the stitch you are working:
Single crochet = 1 chain
Half double crochet = 2 chains
Double crochet = 3 chains
Treble = 4 chains
Work the required stitches to complete the round. At the end of the round, slip stitch into the top of the chain to close the round.

If you work in a spiral you do not need a turning chain. After completing the base ring, place a stitch marker in the first stitch and then continue to crochet around. When you have made a round and reached the point where the stitch marker is, work this stitch, take out the stitch marker from the previous round and put it back into the first stitch of the new round. A safety pin or piece of yarn in a contrasting color makes a good stitch marker.

Making rows

When making straight rows you turn the work at the end of each row and make a turning chain to create the height you need for the stitch you are working with, as for making rounds.
Single crochet = 1 chain
Half double crochet = 2 chains
Double crochet = 3 chains
Treble = 4 chains

Working into top of stitch

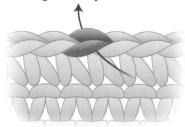

Unless otherwise directed, always insert the hook under both of the two loops on top of the stitch—this is the standard technique.

Working into front loop of stitch (FLO)

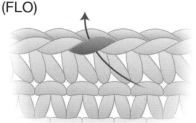

To work into the front loop of a stitch, pick up the front loop from underneath at the front of the work.

Working into back loop of stitch (BLO)

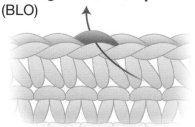

To work into the back loop of the stitch, insert the hook between the front and the back loop, picking up the back loop from the front of the work.

How to measure a gauge (tension) square

Using the hook and the yarn recommended in the pattern, make a number of chains to measure approximately 6in (15cm). Working in the stitch pattern given for the gauge measurements, work enough rows to form a square. Fasten off.

Take a ruler, place it horizontally across the square and, using pins, mark a 4in (10cm) area. Repeat vertically to form a 4in (10cm) square on the fabric.

Count the number of stitches across, and the number of rows within the square, and compare against the gauge given in the pattern.

If your numbers match the pattern then use this size hook and yarn for your project. If you have more stitches, then your gauge is tighter than recommended and you need to use a larger hook. If you have fewer stitches, then your gauge is looser and you will need a smaller hook.

Make gauge squares using different size hooks until you have matched the tension in the pattern, and use this hook to make the project.

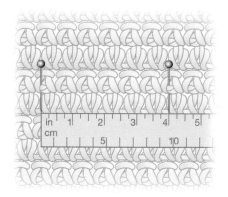

Single crochet (sc)

1 Insert the hook into your work, yarn over hook and pull the yarn through the work only. You will then have 2 loops on the hook.

2 Yarn over hook again and pull through the two loops on the hook. You will then have 1 loop on the hook.

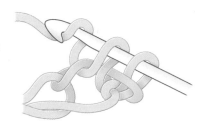

Half double crochet (hdc)

  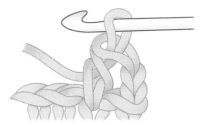

1 Before inserting the hook into the work, wrap the yarn over the hook and put the hook through the work with the yarn wrapped over it.

2 Yarn over hook again and pull through the first loop on the hook. You now have 3 loops on the hook.

3 Yarn over hook and pull the yarn through all 3 loops. You will be left with 1 loop on the hook.

Double crochet (dc)

1 Before inserting the hook into the work, wrap the yarn over the hook. Put the hook through the work with the yarn wrapped over it, yarn over hook again and pull through the first loop on the hook. You now have 3 loops on the hook.

2 Yarn over hook again, pull the yarn through the first 2 loops on the hook. You now have 2 loops on the hook.

3 Pull the yarn through 2 loops again. You will be left with 1 loop on the hook.

Treble (tr)

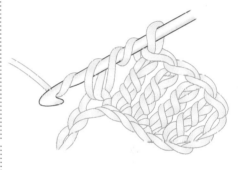

Yarn over hook twice, insert the hook into the stitch, yarn over hook, pull a loop through (4 loops on hook), yarn over hook, pull the yarn through 2 stitches (3 loops on hook), yarn over hook, pull a loop through the next 2 stitches (2 loops on hook), yarn over hook, pull a loop through the last 2 stitches. You will be left with 1 loop on the hook.

Double treble (dtr)

Double trebles are "tall" stitches and are an extension on the basic treble stitch. They need a turning chain of 5 chains.

1 Yarn over hook three times, insert the hook into the stitch or space. Yarn over hook, pull the yarn through the work (5 loops on hook).

2 Yarn over hook, pull the yarn through the first 2 loops on the hook (4 loops on hook).

3 Yarn over hook, pull the yarn through the first 2 loops on the hook (3 loops on hook).

4 Yarn over hook, pull the yarn through the first 2 loops on the hook (2 loops on hook). Yarn over hook, pull the yarn through the 2 loops on the hook. You will be left with 1 loop on the hook.

Bobble

Bobbles are created when working on wrong-side rows and the bobble is then pushed out towards the right-side row. This is a four-double crochet cluster bobble (4dcCL).

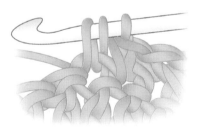

1 Yarn over hook and then insert the hook in the stitch, yarn over hook and pull the yarn through the work.

2 Yarn over hook and pull the yarn through the first 2 loops on the hook (2 loops on hook).

3 Repeat steps 1 and 2 three more times in the same stitch, yarn over hook and pull through all 5 loops on the hook.

4 You can also make 1 chain to complete the bobble.

Increasing

Make two or three stitches into one stitch or space from the previous row. The illustration shows a double crochet increase being made.

Decreasing

You can decrease by either missing the next stitch and continuing to crochet, or by crocheting two or more stitches together. The basic technique for crocheting stitches together is the same, no matter which stitch you are using. The following examples show sc2tog and dc2tog.

SINGLE CROCHET TWO STITCHES TOGETHER (sc2tog)

1 Insert the hook into your work, yarn over hook and pull the yarn through the work (2 loops on hook). Insert the hook in next stitch, yarn over hook and pull the yarn through.

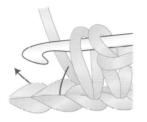

2 Yarn over hook again and pull through all 3 loops on the hook. You will then have 1 loop on the hook.

DOUBLE CROCHET TWO STITCHES TOGETHER (dc2tog)

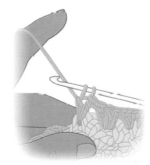

1 Yarn over hook, insert the hook into the next space, yarn over hook, pull the yarn through the work (3 loops on hook).

2 Yarn over hook, pull the yarn through 2 loops on the hook (2 loops on hook).

3 Yarn over hook, insert the hook into the next space.

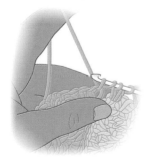

4 Yarn over hook, pull the yarn through the work (4 loops on hook).

5 Yarn over hook, pull the yarn through 2 loops on the hook (3 loops on hook).

6 Yarn over hook, pull the yarn through all 3 loops on the hook (1 loop on hook).

Joining yarn at the end of a row or round

You can use this technique when changing color, or when joining in a new ball
of yarn as one runs out.

1 Keep the loop of the old
yarn on the hook. Drop the
tail and catch a loop of the
strand of the new yarn with
the crochet hook.

2 Draw the new yarn through
the loop on the hook, keeping
the old loop drawn tight and
continue as instructed in the
pattern.

Joining in new yarn after fastening off

1 Fasten off the old color
(see page 123). Make a slip
knot with the new color (see
page 115). Insert the hook
into the stitch at the
beginning of the next row,
then through the slip knot.

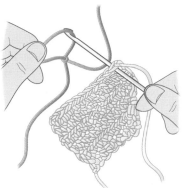

2 Draw the loop of the slip
knot through to the front of
the work. Carry on working
using the new color,
following the instructions
in the pattern.

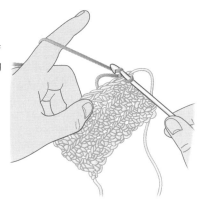

Joining yarn in the middle of a row or round

For a neat color join in the middle of a row or round, use these
methods.

JOINING A NEW COLOR INTO SINGLE CROCHET

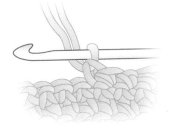
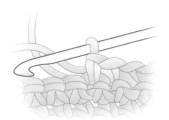

1 Make a single crochet
stitch (see page 118), but
do not draw the final loop
through, so there are 2 loops
on the hook. Drop the old
yarn, catch the new yarn with
the hook and draw it through
both loops to complete the
stitch and join in the new
color at the same time.

2 Continue to crochet with
the new yarn. Cut the old
yarn leaving a 6in (15cm) tail
and weave the tail in (see
right) after working a row, or
once the work is complete.

JOINING A NEW COLOR INTO DOUBLE CROCHET

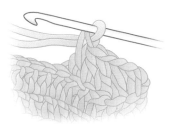
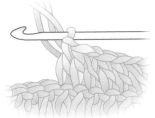

1 Make a double crochet
stitch (see page 119), but
do not draw the final loop
through, so there are 2 loops
on the hook. Drop the old
yarn, catch the new yarn with
the hook and draw it through
both loops to complete the
stitch and join in the new
color at the same time.

2 Continue to crochet with
the new yarn. Cut the old
yarn leaving a 6in (15cm) tail
and weave the tail in (see
right) after working a row, or
once the work is complete.

Enclosing a yarn tail

You may find that the yarn end gets in the way as you work; you can enclose this into the stitches as you go by placing the end at the back as you wrap the yarn. This also saves having to sew this yarn end in later.

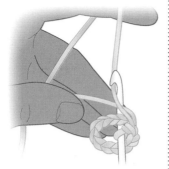

Fastening off

When you have finished crocheting, you need to fasten off the stitches to stop all your work unraveling.

1 Draw up the final loop of the last stitch to make it bigger. Cut the yarn, leaving an end of approximately 4in (10cm)—unless a longer end is needed for sewing up. Pull the end all the way through the loop and pull the loop up tightly.

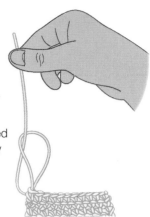

Weaving in yarn ends

It is important to weave in the tail ends of the yarn so that they are secure and your crochet won't unravel. Thread a yarn needle with the yarn end. On the wrong side, take the needle through the crochet one stitch down on the edge, then take it through the stitches, working in a gentle zig-zag. Work through four or five stitches then return in the opposite direction. Remove the needle, pull the crochet gently to stretch it and trim the end.

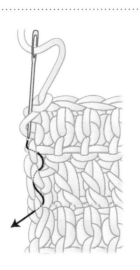

Making a French knot

Bring the needle up from the back of the fabric to the front. Wrap the thread two or three times around the tip of the needle, then reinsert the needle at the point where it first emerged, holding the wrapped threads with the thumbnail of your non-stitching hand, and pull the needle all the way through. The wraps will form a knot on the surface of the fabric.

Blocking

When making wreaths and garlands you will find that taking the time to block and stiffen each crochet element will make a huge difference to the finished effect of your work. Without either of these processes you will find that the crochet will curl out of shape and lose its definition.

For a quick and easy way to block your crochet you'll need blocking pins, some soft foam mats (such as the ones sold as children's play mats) and some ironing spray starch. Pin each item out to shape and size onto the mats and then spray with the starch. Allow to dry for a day before attaching the elements to your wreath or garland.

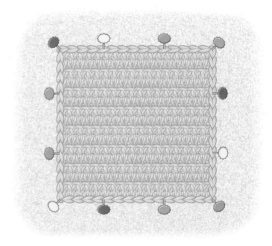

Making an oversewn seam

An oversewn join gives a nice flat seam and is the simplest and most common joining technique.

 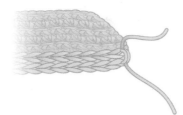 

1 Thread a yarn sewing needle with the yarn you're using in the project. Place the pieces to be joined with right sides together.

2 Insert the needle in one corner in the top loops of the stitches of both pieces and pull up the yarn, leaving a tail of about 2in (5cm). Go into the same place with the needle and pull up the yarn again; repeat two or three times to secure the yarn at the start of the seam.

3 Join the pieces together by taking the needle through the loops at the top of corresponding stitches on each piece to the end. Fasten off the yarn at the end, as in step 2.

Making a single crochet seam

With a single crochet seam you join two pieces together using a crochet hook and working a single crochet stitch through both pieces, instead of sewing them together with a tail of yarn and a yarn sewing needle. This makes a quick and strong seam and gives a slightly raised finish to the edging. For a less raised seam, follow the same basic technique, but work each stitch in slip stitch rather than single crochet.

1 Start by lining up the two pieces with wrong sides together. Insert the hook in the top 2 loops of the stitch of the first piece, then into the corresponding stitch on the second piece.

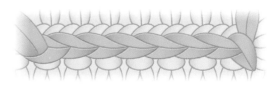

2 Complete the single crochet stitch as normal and continue on the next stitches as directed in the pattern. This gives a raised effect if the single crochet stitches are made on the right side of the work.

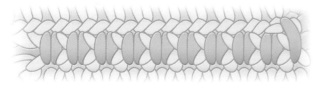

3 You can work with the wrong side of the work facing (with the pieces right side facing) if you don't want this effect and it still creates a good strong join.

Making a garland base

A garland base can be made from any number of things, such as twisted branches, a thick piece of rope, or a length of fabric twisted and held with florist's wire. However, one of the best methods I have found is to use lengths of raffia combined with florist's wire. This method gives a very lightweight base that can be moulded to the shape that you want, and you can easily attach the crochet elements using a needle and thread. Raffia can be purchased either online or from hobby stores and it comes in a range of different colors. For a garland approximately 60in (150cm) long when finished, I use three 2oz (50g) packs of raffia and a roll of florist's wire.

Begin by taking the lengths of raffia out of the packets and carefully teasing the strands into long, straight lengths. Take one of the lengths and carefully attach the florist's wire tightly around one end to secure it. Begin twisting the raffia and the wire together, working your way down the length of raffia and wrapping the wire tightly around it as you twist.

As you work your way along the raffia you will find the garland will become a little thinner as you get towards the end of the strand. At this point bring in the next length of raffia and carry on in the same way until you have combined all three lengths of raffia into one long length. Add extra wire if there are parts that seem to need extra support. Trim all along the garland to neaten, then turn over a hanging loop at each end of the raffia and secure in place with more florist's wire.

You can either hang your garland as one curving length, or you can create a series of swags by bending the wire and raffia where appropriate. When attaching the crochet elements to the garland it's best to use a needle and thread as—by its nature—the garland is designed to be fairly flexible and sewing will allow for a bit more movement than if the items are attached using a hot glue gun.

Making a wreath

There are a wide range of wreaths available to buy, either online, in hobby stores or from a florist's, but it's also easy to make your own. For a wreath approximately 12in (30cm) in diameter when finished, you will need two 2oz (50g) packs of raffia and a roll of florist's wire.

Follow the instructions for the garland, but only using two lengths of raffia. When you are finished, secure the ends together with florist's wire to make a ring shape.

When attaching the crochet elements to your wreath, it's best to use a hot glue gun.

Hanging garlands and wreaths

Hanging up a garland or displaying a wreath is such a quick way to add an instant change to your home décor, whether it's to welcome in a new season or to add decoration for festivals and celebrations. Garlands work particularly well hung below a mantelpiece or shelf, whether it's above a fireplace, in a bedroom, or even in the kitchen. They work equally well strung along bannisters of a staircase—and if you are lucky enough to have a house full of beams, the world is your oyster! Wreaths are very versatile and can be hung anywhere and everywhere, from a wall, to a door, to a gate. They also work equally well as stand-alone ornaments positioned on a shelf, mantelpiece, or dressing table.

I find the best way to secure a garland is by attaching a small hanging loop, made with either string or thin wire, at the back at each end. If your garland is divided into swags just add further loops where needed to support the shape.

The hanging loop for a wreath can be hidden away at the back by attaching a loop of string or wire. Alternatively, the loop can be very much a part of the design, perhaps worked in coordinating ribbon and big enough to be seen over the top of the wreath.

Storage

Wreaths and garlands can be stored by wrapping them in acid-free tissue paper and carefully packing them into a box.

CROCHET STITCH CONVERSION CHART

Crochet stitches are worked in the same way in both the UK and the USA, but the stitch names are not the same and identical names are used for different stitches. Below is a list of the UK terms used in this book, and the equivalent US terms.

US TERM	UK TERM
single crochet (sc)	double crochet (dc)
half double crochet (hdc)	half treble (htr)
double crochet (dc)	treble (tr)
treble (tr)	double treble (dtr)
double treble (dtr)	triple treble (ttr)
triple treble (ttr)	quadruple treble (qtr)
gauge	tension
yarn over hook (yoh)	yarn round hook (yrh)

abbreviations

alt	alternat(e)ing
approx.	approximately
beg	beginning
BLO	back loop only
cm	centimeter(s)
cont	continu(e)ing
ch	chain
dc	double crochet
dc2tog	double crochet 2 stitches together
dec	decreas(e)ing
dtr	double treble
FLO	front loop only
foll	follow(s)ing
g	gram(mes)
htr	half treble
in	inch(es)
inc	increas(e)ing
m	meter(s)
mm	millimeter(s)
oz	ounce(s)
PM	place marker
prev	previous
rem	remaining
rep	repeat
RS	right side
sc	single crochet
sl st	slip stitch
st(s)	stitch(es)
tog	together
tr	treble
yds	yards
WS	wrong side
yoh	yarn over hook
[ ]	work section between square brackets number of times stated
*	asterisk indicates beginning of repeated section of pattern

suppliers

For reasons of space we cannot cover all stockists, so please explore the local yarn shops and online stores in your own country.

USA

Knitting Fever Inc.
www.knittingfever.com

WEBS
www.yarn.com

Jo-Ann Fabric and Craft Stores
Yarns and craft supplies
www.joann.com

Michaels
Craft supplies
www.michaels.com

UK

Love Crochet
Online sales
www.lovecrochet.com

Wool
Yarn, hooks
Store in Bath.
+44 (0)1225 469144
www.woolbath.co.uk

VV Rouleaux
Ribbons
Stores in London and Bath, UK.
+44 (0)1225 618600
www.vvrouleaux.com

Deramores
Online sales
www.deramores.com

Laughing Hens
Online sales
Tel: +44 (0) 1829 740903
www.laughinghens.com

John Lewis
Yarns and craft supplies
Telephone numbers of stores on website
www.johnlewis.com

Hobbycraft
Twig wreath bases and raffia
www.hobbycraft.co.uk

AUSTRALIA

Black Sheep Wool 'n' Wares
Retail store and online
Tel: +61 (0)2 6779 1196
www.blacksheepwool.com.au

Sun Spun
Retail store only
(Canterbury, Victoria)
Tel: +61 (0)3 9830 1609

YARN COMPANIES

Cascade
Stockist locator on website
www.cascadeyarns.com

DMC
Stockist locator on website
www.dmc.com

Rowan Yarns
Stockist locator on website
www.knitrowan.com

If you wish to substitute a different yarn for the one recommended in the pattern, try the **Yarnsub** website for suggestions:
www.yarnsub.com

acknowledgments

My acknowledgments have to start with an enormous thank you to everyone at CICO books who has helped me to realize my dream of sitting with a crochet book in front of me that I have written. Cindy Richards, Penny Craig and their wonderful team have made the whole experience an absolute pleasure from start to finish and I simply cannot put into words how delighted I am with the finished book—from the editing to the styling to the photography, every little detail is totally perfect and more than I could have ever hoped for. Thank you!

When I was asked if I would like to write a book featuring designs for 35 different crocheted wreaths and garlands my first thought was how I would ever be able to come up with that many ideas. As it turned out, once I got started, I found myself having to rein the ideas in and stay focused on the job in hand. But—and it's a very big but—I could not have done any of it without all the amazing support that I had around me and so I have some enormous thank yous to say.

First to Meg, my eldest daughter, who has held the fort magnificently at our Nursery School whilst I have been absent from my desk. Thank you, Meg. I could not have accepted this opportunity without you behind me.

Secondly to Beth, my middle daughter, who not only provided me with a big bag full of book-writing materials but then sent regular care packages of chocolate and biscuits through the post, which always seemed to arrive just when I needed them the most. Thank you, Beth.

Thirdly to Immi, my youngest daughter, who would turn up at the back door and fly through the house like a dynamo cleaning things, sorting, tidying, hoovering and generally digging me out from under my pile of crochet. Thank you, Immi.

And then to Dave, my husband, who, whilst staying calm and under no pressure whatsoever, has been quite magnificent in his ability to guess correctly every time a random crochet item has been held aloft with those dreaded words "what does that look like?" I thank you, Dave.

A very big thank you to my friends at lovecrochet.com who have not only supported me so much in my crochet designing over the past three years but provided all of the delicious yarn needed to create each and every one of the wreaths and garlands for this book.

I would also like to thank the many wonderful friends that I have made on my crochet journey, who have been a constant source of encouragement and support throughout the years.

And finally, I would like to thank my Mum who started me off on this wonderful crafting road all those years ago, and my Dad who, from my earliest years, instilled in me the love of a good book.

index